Praise for Adam Cox

"I was overweight, stressed and supposedly on life-long medication. I have been seeing Adam for around a year and a half now and the difference he has made to my life is incredible. He doesn't just give you a schedule to follow but also educates you and this is knowledge you have for life. I have not taken my medication for almost a year and feel absolutely great."

M Kkafas

"I have had major spinal surgery twice and complicated post surgical difficulties. I had trouble in basic movement and after months of rehabilitation and bed rest, I developed problems with my muscle strength and knock-on issues.

Since working with Adam I have a far more active lifestyle and am becoming more confident in my enhanced range of movement. I feel increasingly confident to know I will have much better physical movement in the future without doing further damage, and I am far more aware of my ability now."

S Waxkirsh

"I am in a lot less pain on a daily basis and my back is as good as it has ever been. My overall strength and general health are far superior to before. Considering my medical history, my work and lifestyle all this improvement is quite remarkable. This is in no small part down to Adam's influence, training and advice."

B Conway

"Adam is wise beyond his years, totally dedicated to what he does and very much lives what he preaches. His depth and understanding of human nature and health and fitness is extraordinary. I find him inspiring and his positivity is infectious. In terms of nutrition and health he has helped me transform myself."

Simon Urwin

"I've always done sport and weight training. His approach is like nothing I've seen. His approach is not like others trainers out there. I've learned a huge amount."

G Kauffman

"Adam is a real expert in his field. He understands human health and wellbeing deeply, practically, mindfully and holistically. His rounded approach to fitness and health puts him at the top of his profession. He is truly a specialist in helping people excel in mind, body and spirit. I'm very glad he was recommended to me and I would recommend him to anyone. My advice is you better benefit from his expertise before the queue becomes too long!"

R Ogunlaru

"I've been to other top specialists before, such as physiotherapists and chiropractors, but Adam involves you in a way that's engaging and that makes it easier to understand."

James Booth

"Adam excels and leads by example inspiring real change. He works by treating the body as a whole system and finding the root cause of a problem, which in turn produces long term results. I have great confidence in his work and ability to give a personalised holistic corrective exercise program."

A Eaton

BACK TO BRILLIANT!

A five step method to more energy,
a better body and fewer aches and pains.

ADAM COX

WRITING MATTERS PUBLISHING

Back to Brilliant:
A five step method to more energy, a better body and fewer aches and pains.

Copyright 2016 Adam Cox

First published in 2016

Writing Matters Publishing, Kent UK
info@writingmatterspublishing.com
www.writingmatterspublishing.com

Illustrations: Andrew Priestley

ISBN 978-0-9956051-0-7

This book is available to order online from Amazon worldwide.

Please note: This book is intended as information only and does not constitute specific health, physical or emotional advice unique to your situation. The Author, Publisher and Resellers accept no responsibility for loss, damage or injury to persons or their belongings as a direct or indirect result of reading this book.

Dedication

To all clients, past and present, who were bold enough to take charge of their health, fitness and wellbeing and for their feedback that shaped my ideas:

To Lynne and Clive Collins, Paul and Carol Cox, Simon Urwin, Steve Briginshaw and Paul Allen for their tremendous love, support and friendship;

To Ian James, Michael Symons, Tracey Burnette and Georgia Kaufmann, the clients who took the extra time to listen to my ideas and gave invaluable input;

To Chris and Carol Beskin for the use of their office space, where the quiet little sanctuary brought cohesion to a bunch of disparate ideas, with Leo the cat for company;

To my mentors, Paul Chek, Matthew Wallden, JP Sears and Aaron Mckenzie who, in a world full of experts, are the real deal. Thank you.

And special dedication to my partner, Hannah Beskin. Without your love and amazing support this book might never have seen the light of day.

I give you the biggest thank you of all!

Contents

Back to Brilliant at a glance

Unfit, out of shape and in chronic pain

Back To Brilliant is the result of years of successfully working with clients who are unfit, out of shape and who suffer from chronic neck, shoulder and back pain.

Typically Adam's clients are time-poor executives and business owners who have struggles to incorporate health into their busy schedules. Importantly, they have tried just about everything to get fit, stay in shape and be pain-free.

The 5R Method

Adam Cox, an ex-elite athlete, is a qualified and highly experienced personal trainer who has developed a unique method for making lasting positive physical changes called *The 5R Method* that includes *Reconnect, Rebalance, Realign, Rebuild* and *Recover*. It is a substantial, holistic approach that combines the practical, physical, mental, emotional and spiritual.

100-Day Transformations

Adam specifically designs *100-Day Transformations* for his personal clients. *Back To Brilliant* explains the key principles he successfully incorporates into these bespoke programmes.

Who should read *Back to Brilliant*?

If you are already fit, in shape and pain-free you will find *Back to Brilliant* an invaluable resource that distills Adam's long experience in achieving peak fitness and health. This book will add important distinctions to your current regime.

If you are unfit, out of shape and in chronic pain *Back to Brilliant* will definitely provide an important platform for designing a far more effective health and fitness programme that addresses why our best intentions to achieve a healthier lifestyle are often doomed to fail.

More information on the web

In addition to this book there is a wealth of information available on Adam's business website.

Movement Lifestyle is a successful holistic health and fitness practice based in London, UK dedicated to negotiating clients challenges with chronic pain or body shape transformation using advanced techniques in nutrition and lifestyle coaching, functional and corrective exercise and mindfulness strategies.

Please discover more at:

www.movementlifestyle.com

About Adam Cox

Adam is an experienced holistic health and fitness coach with qualifications from the *Chek Institute* (USA). His mission is to show you how to achieve a healthy, beautiful, pain-free body and mind.

He believes that *to lead by example* is the only way to achieve real change and inspire people.

The simplicity of the tools that Adam lives by and coaches with are based on his formal training, personal challenges and feedback from each client he has coached.

He specialises in the inner game and has refined an approach that counteracts negative internal dialogue and self-sabotage that is often at the root of programmes that under-perform, stall or fail.

Introduction

Do you have lower back pain? Are your energy levels less than you'd like them to be from time to time, or all the time? Would you like to feel and look stronger? Sleep better? And most importantly, would you like to feel a sense of inner peace? This book will take you back to feeling Brilliant, inside and out.

Think back to a time when you were feeling brilliant. Stop for a second and think back right now. Remember a moment when you were in peak flow, relationships were great, health was great, finances as you wanted them and the world was a great place. Who were you with? What were you doing? How much or how little stress did you feel? There was no back, neck or other body pain, energy was plentiful and you looked as good as you ever had.

In the next few pages we'll uncover what the secrets were to that peak state, why it felt so good and how you can be at your peak more often from this day forward.

This is a holistic approach and may encourage you to embrace aspects that you wouldn't at first connect to your current health and fitness challenges. Ultimately though, the whole is often greater than the sum of its parts and therefore, we must embrace the whole and how that whole works in unison to improve your function, physically, mentally, emotionally and dare I say it, that most taboo of words, spiritually!

How this book is structured

In Part 1, I'll share some of the common challenges that I see most people face when trying to make changes to their health and wellbeing and trying to find relief from long term aches and pains.

In Part 2, I'll give you the five step methodology we use in the Movement Lifestyle practice to coach our clients to successful results and finally in Part 3, some ideas for bringing the theory to life!

My Story

I run *Movement Lifestyle*, a holistic health and fitness coaching practice based in London, UK. We deliver 100 day transformation programmes for men and women 40 and over who want more energy, a better body and fewer aches and pains.

My sporting background is elite level swimming and the 100 meters butterfly was my chosen stroke. At my peak I was training 6-8 times per week and at 12-13 years old I was determined to make it to the top in my sport.

However I began to suffer with debilitating stomach pains that would stop me from training and eating.

After 10 years of seeing doctors, having scans and numerous tests, a specialist believed it was necessary for me to have gall bladder surgery. Unfortunately the operation wasn't the solution because following surgery I still had the symptoms plus an extensive recovery period. Basically I stopped swimming at that point and it left a huge hole in my life. I spent the next few years trying to find myself and discover what I was good at and what I could focus on now swimming was no longer my goal.

It lead me to explore optimal health and wellbeing. I began by studying sports massage therapy and eventually it lead me to studying with the Chek Institute based in San Diego, California. They're world leaders in corrective exercise and holistic health.

I became fascinated by how people would respond to certain techniques such as massage therapy and how others wouldn't. Why people would feel benefit for a short time then revert to their old state within days of receiving my treatments. I was frustrated without answers, however I wanted to help others understand their challenges, not just with a quick fix but by digging deep into the root causes.

At this stage of my career I could never have predicted the journey ahead. Through study with the Chek Institute and learning from mentors I've gained awareness of the roots of my challenges and how to manage myself each day so I can thrive and extract the most from life.

To finally understand my phantom stomach pains I had to become aware of my emotions! This didn't come naturally at first. As you'll read later in the book, every organ you have shares connections with the muscles of your body. And each organ has related emotions. Trapped emotions that need to be expressed but are in fact repressed mean the body has to do something with the resulting energy. In my case it was letting me know about repressed anger in the form of pain in the region of my gallbladder and liver.

The most important lesson I've learnt is that I possess ability far beyond what I imagine, as do you. It might yet be an untapped source, a wellspring of potential hidden inside but it's there!

Your journey will be unique to you; the roots may be more of a physical nature, a nutritional nature or like mine a mixture of physical, nutritional and emotional. I invite you to keep an open mind while reading and if something challenges your current thinking, it could be tapping into your hidden potential you've been suppressing. Why would you do that?

I hope you find freedom from long term aches and pains, abundant energy, fitness and vitality, deeper sleep and even deeper levels of contentment.

Part 1

The Challenges You Face

The 95% Failure Rate

Have you ever set a goal or made a New Year's Resolution and failed to achieve it? Have you reset a goal and then failed to achieve that as well? Have you tried to lose weight and not managed to, or done so then put the weight back on again? Then you'll know what I mean.

However it can be any goal, to get rid of back pain, exercise more consistently, get a higher paying job or a simple habit such as getting to bed a little earlier each night.

Goals make an interesting topic.

There are so many goal setting experts who claim to have the answer to achieving all you ever wanted, all you could ever dream. And it appears all you have to do is set the goal and be disciplined, then "hey-presto" the new car, dream body or dream relationship appears before your eyes! That's not how it happens for me and believe me I've tried.

In fact looking at the statistics for the number of people who struggle to achieve their goals, in respect of their health and fitness, is rather worrying.

In a workshop on *Living Beyond Self Sabotage* with JP Sears he referenced a statistic for the number of people failing to achieve their goals in the health and fitness industry as 95%!

Does that sound like something is going wrong to you?

That figure represents either a lot of people with poor self-discipline or the way we are looking at achieving the goals isn't working. I'm willing to place money on the fact there is a bit of both to blame. However discipline and method can both be remedied when you delve into why you might sabotage your own best efforts.

I've discovered that even highly motivated - and often very successful, disciplined people - self sabotage. And in my opinion self sabotage is the best explanation for why their previous programmes failed.

Self Sabotage

So what is *self sabotage*?

- *Self sabotage* is a form of inner conflict
- *Self sabotage* is a validation of unresolved emotional wounds or disempowering beliefs about yourself
- *Self sabotage* is hoping for things to be different from how they actually are, right now!

If you experience inner conflict, either consciously on unconsciously towards a goal, it provides resistance. The greater the resistance you have the more likely you are to fail in achieving your goals in the long term.

Discipline can carry you through the resistance at first but, just as a moth finds the light, you are likely to be attracted back to the unresolved emotional wounds in your psyche. The question is, at what point can you take your self-discipline guard down? When it falls down due to fatigue?

An alternative approach to goal setting might be to embrace what it is that provides the potential resistance in the first place, therefore making the resistance smaller and your journey to goal achievement easier. The energy required to be disciplined can now be spent enjoying your life, as it's not needed any longer for the tussle between two or more conflicted ego parts, which were gaining some benefit from the tussle. The result is maintaining the status quo and therefore not achieving your desired outcome.

Client Story

About five years ago I worked with a client who was initially enthusiastic about us working together. He had decided his fast-paced career and busy social life needed to be supported by some healthy habits and some of the old unhealthy ones knocked on the head. He had intermittent lower back pain, was overweight and had bags under his eyes from long work days, late nights and poor sleep.

He mentioned that he had been to gyms before, tried a number of different diets and nothing really seemed to work for him, but this time he was so fed up with how unhealthy he was feeling that he'd decided enough was enough and he meant business!

He stuck rigidly to the exercise programme and dietary changes for nearly three weeks when he missed a gym session. His eating habits then began to revert back to how they were before the new declaration to 'a healthy new me' and within another week, he had manage to miss all his training sessions and put some of the weight back on that he had managed to lose.

After another two weeks the new regime had hit the rocks and he'd succumbed to the invisible force of self-sabotage.

In part 2 you will see the SUCCESS Goal Setting approach I use with my coaching clients to enable them to achieve goals with less effort and prevent such a relapse.

A friend once said, we can take a picture or look in a mirror to reflect our physical attributes back to us so we can see ourselves but there are no emotional cameras.

The emotional camera you do have is the world and people around you. That might be quite scary at first to sit with? You might think, "Okay but I hate my current body shape and you're telling me its my emotions?" or "I'm having a really tough time at work and that's all my fault?" or "My back pain is because of my emotions?" These are not facts but would you be willing to consider them as possibilities?

In short self-sabotage is a way for the inner conflicted parts of your mind to express themselves on your outer world to gain acceptance or validation. In the previous client story, part of him wanted to make those changes and feel better and yet another part of him wanted to break that commitment. The tussle between the two parts of his mind stopped him dead in his tracks.

This scenario can manifest itself in many areas of your life such as:

- Emotional eating
- Body pains
- Fatigue
- Poor libido
- Excess body weight
- Mood swings
- Ill health
- Turbulent relationships
- Inability to reach goals
- Laziness
- Financial stress
- Taking on too much

You don't keep repeating your behaviours or keep issues in your life unless there is a benefit to some part of you. Where would you guess you sabotage yourself most? What would you imagine is the benefit to that sabotage in your life?

Excess Body Weight As Sabotage

Are you overweight? Have you tried diets? Training hard? Working with trainers? Juicing cleanses and detox programmes and nothing seems to work for you?

Do you even go through spells of training really well and being disciplined with preparing foods but ultimately lapse after a while, back to your comfortable habits, especially if life gets stressful in other areas.

There may be some people who seem to have it easy when it comes to managing a healthy weight and appearing vibrant (which is very different to just being thin).

They eat well most of the time but enjoy some things you might regard as unhealthy, exercise but not excessively, work hard, have family responsibilities and still they seem to look great and have plenty of energy! What are they doing differently and why can't you seem to strike that balance? It must be that they are incredibly disciplined. They know something you don't. They just have good genes! All of the above?

Maybe they experience less stress? The fight/flight response can be activated by a level of emotional stress far less than you would imagine, so although you may not think there is much stress in your outer world, your biology reacts as though there is, increasing a key stress hormone, cortisol, and decreasing growth hormones.

When you have an emotional fight/flight response due to a lack of inner peace and harmony you can lose muscle and increase fat tissue, decreasing your chance of losing weight no matter how hard you work in the gym or how well you eat.

Furthermore, not only will you struggle to lose weight if you exercise when you're body is predominantly in a fight/flight state but you are likely to increase body fat.

The table on the next page shows the reactions that take place within, when there are levels of emotional stress, in comparison to a balanced emotional state.

If you're aware of any of the symptoms in the column on the left, you are experiencing some form of stress and it could be rooted in your emotions.

Increased Emotional Stress	Decreased Emotional Stress
Fat building	Fat burning
Increased stress hormone - cortisol	Increased metabolic hormone - growth hormone
Decreased lean muscle	Increased lean muscle
Decreased metabolic rate	Increased metabolic rate
Poor digestive function	Improved digestive function
Increased fungal infections	Adequate levels of bacteria in the gut

Back Pain As Sabotage

Do you suffer with lower back pain?

Have you tried physiotherapists, chiropractors and osteopaths or even Pilates classes and nothing really worked for you long term? Does it bug you that you can't do simple movements when your back is painful, like picking up your children or kicking a ball around with them?

You may have also had people show you techniques and modifications that will help you improve your alignment and the function of your lower back and hips, yet you don't do them?

You may not do them consistently or you eat foods that you know give you bloating and gas, weakening your abdomen and therefore taking support away from your back?

This may be a perfect strategy for your inner saboteur to poke its head up and be noticed, AKA you noticing another part of yourself.

If you didn't go through the cycle how would that part of you get its needs met?

Your back could well be trying to teach you about part of your psyche you've been repressing, for fear of contacting painful wounds.

Working Too Much As Sabotage

Why would you choose to work so much that you become exhausted and worn out? So burnt out that each morning when your alarm goes off you feel groggy, hung over even!

It takes a shower and hot drink to feel human and then, off you go to repeat the frantic pace of yesterday all over again. And the weekend doesn't allow you the chance to catch up on rest; the kids need to be taken to football practice, gymnastics and swimming club and there are emails to catch up on from the week.

Are you scrambling to reach a sense of being on top of work when you can relax? When you have the job title and the pay to meet your financial needs you'll slow down a little, when you have the house and car you'll step back and start to enjoy life more.

Your mantra for working too much as a form of sabotage might sound something like: "I need to keep pushing until I get to… then I can change my lifestyle and relax a little".

How long have you been saying that?

Does that point seem to get closer or does that magical moment in your mind seem to be within touching distance, but never quite arrives?

What would your life be like if you got to this elusive point right now? How much better would life be? What advantages would you have over what you experience currently? Would there be less stress? More free time? Would you feel more at ease with life? Be able to roll with the challenges as they arise and smile a bit more?

While your situation may not be exactly like this, it might well be somewhere close.

I assume there are people you know, or maybe even envy, who seem to be super busy and seem to be getting more tasks ticked off their 'to do list' but they don't look worn out; they seem to be having fun and living life. They manage to balance their commitments with a bit of 'me time'. If they're business owners they start when they want to, get things done and manage a team effectively so they can get away at a reasonable time and get to the gym in the evening to look after their health and fitness.

They seem to be thriving and love the life they have created for themselves. If they are employed, they have a good job position that allows them the flexibility to fit their personal lives around their work commitments and they enjoy benefits that the company offers them.

I suggest that you work so hard because you get a sense of purpose from working hard. You try to manage everything and be in control. If you're the head of a team, you strive to help other team members, even doing their work for them and 'rescuing' them. Your team is like your little family away from your family and your sense of purpose is validated by the fact they need you. You like to be busy and you like to be needed. If there is a crisis, part of your psyche can't wait to jump in and help solve it because while you know the long workdays and lack of weekends off will feel like hell, you'll get the praise and recognition you crave in some part of your psyche you might not even be aware of.

This scenario contradicts your core values, however, as you love to feel fresh, get great exercise and eat well.

You love to spend time with friends and family and read your favourite books. Sitting in your garden or in the park on a Sunday afternoon; there's nothing better. But when you're working so hard all you want is a coffee, a can of coke or some sugar to keep you riding the adrenaline high to make sure you 'get stuff done!'

Remember one of the definitions of self-sabotage is form of inner conflict. Could it be true for you that a part of you bene-fits from being needed in a crisis but part of you detests giving up on your values to solve that crisis? Could this be an inner sense of conflict? What would it mean to you if this clash was happening subconsciously without you even knowing? The only thing you *know* is that life is not as free flowing as it should be.

Taking Too Much On As Sabotage

Why do you like to fill up your diary? Do you feel that your diary should be full to feel like you're getting somewhere and making the most of life?

Taking on new projects and interests can be exciting as the "newness" helps to get over feelings of disconnection and boredom. Something new though requires extra energy and anxiety in tackling the unfamiliar.

However why do you sometimes take on several new projects at once, only to get a few weeks or months down the line and feel overloaded. There's too much to manage and you're not doing any of them as well as you'd like to. At first you get the buzz from trying new activities like playing a new sport, a new hobby, a new job.

However do you ever notice that once you're really busy with your new interests that you've actually dropped the ball with some of them? You might then feel you need to relinquish some of these activities as there's too much on your plate! And you need some breathing space to just relax and enjoy free time!

You might notice that you go through cycles. You have a few months of a lull, then all of a sudden you get excited about taking on new challenges and off you go, full steam ahead until you're exhausted and life forces you to rest, in the way of illness or a energy slump or fit of depression or resentment.

Why would you over load yourself like that? What is the downside of over-doing it? How do you feel about yourself when you drop the ball on some of your commitments? How do you benefit from feeling like this?

Have a look at the martyr cycle. You can place any form of sabotage at the beginning of that cycle. You might find you have different types of sabotage for different areas of your life.

Following your sabotaging behaviours you may punish yourself for doing failing at something that seemed so simple; you then feel sorry for yourself and ultimately this cycle culminates in you getting to notice your deeper self. You notice your feelings, good, bad or otherwise. You notice the self talk and the friction. It's a perfect cycle for part of your mind to be recognised and validated. Would you be willing to see self-sabotage as a blessing as much as a curse?

Sabotage self

NOTICE SELF!

Punish self

Feel sorry for yourself

The Martyr Cycle

The Cycles of Self Sabotage

When looking at self sabotage it's possible to see patterns.

You might go through varying peaks and troughs. Some cycles can be weekly, for example, you drink too much at the weekend, wake up and punish yourself, you feel sorry for yourself for feeling worse-for-wear then make a pact to abstain for a while or drink less next time. You stay away from alcohol all week then repeat the process in a major or minor way the following weekend. You might have a similar pattern over a longer period of months.

Your cycles might be with food instead of alcohol, volatile relationships or roller coaster feelings. Whatever your issue, what is your cycle of self sabotage and how does the cycle look?

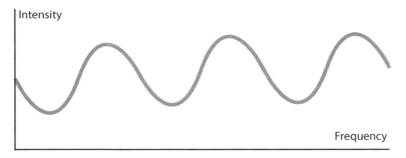

Intensity and Frequency of Recurring Sabotage

You might recognise the rhythm of your cycle. Each sabotage cycle has an ascension phase, crest, descent and trough.

JP Sears says the ascension phase is when you're building toward experiencing what you call your sabotage. He says you may have little or no awareness that you're ascending right into the dragon's cave.

The ascension phase is an infrastructure of beliefs, feelings, attitudes and possibly behaviours that support the peak of sabotage, much like an ocean wave has a body to support its peak.

"You may associate the infrastructure of the ascension phase with positivity and hope or you may experience the opposite polarity of negativity and hopelessness. In other words, our ascension phase may tend to set us up to be blind sided by the hatching of our sabotage egg or it may leave us seeing it coming."

Much like the client story I shared, the ascension phase of his sabotage was the enthusiasm and motivation to make drastic changes to his lifestyle, followed by the sabotage to those plans and the fall down the wave on the other side, where he felt depressed, guilty and ashamed that, again he hadn't managed to make the changes he so desperately wanted.

So far you've read about goal setting and the poor results people are having with achieving them. You've seen how this can be rooted in an emotional nature and you hopefully have seen how that plays out for you from time to time.

Another source of challenges you might face, like many of my clients, is lower back pain.

Lower Back Pain

Do you suffer with lower back pain? Have you ever suffered? If not you could in the future, unfortunately.

The World Health Organization suggests that 80% of the world population will experience lower back at least once in their lives and that half of those will go on to have long term problems.

Would you believe that 75% of the western population has undiagnosed disk bulges? That is, the disks are not in an ideal state yet they are not causing symptoms for the time being. Is this a ticking time bomb?

The average age for an L5/S1 disk bulge (the disk level with your belt line) in males is 32. If you're older then the chances are your spine will have some signs of wear and tear already.

Contributing factors to lower back pain can be wide ranging and complex however there are some common factors that I come across with clients:

- Poor posture
- Poor ergonomics (home, office, car)
- Poorly designed exercise programmes
- Diets that stress the digestive system
- Stress (mental/emotional)
- Long term dehydration
- Lack of movement

Lower back pain might be scary for you. It could pose a risk to your future physical independence, happiness and freedom. It might well be severely limiting your activities, especially if you're fearful of having a relapse of previous aches and pains.

Have you reached into the boot of your car to grab a bag and your back went into spasm, leaving you unable to move properly for days afterwards? Your most risky movement might be putting socks and shoes on, something that you do with caution, just in case your back goes again!

Is It Actually Your Back?

Is it actually your back that's the problem; the root of the issue? Or do you think there could be an alternative explanation? An even deeper meaning to your back pain?

My clients usually have insidious back pain. It comes on, under the radar, over a period of time and then results in long term aches and pains.

Due to the nature of this type of pain there are usually many other things that are out of balance, aside from simply having sporadic back pain.

Commonly you might also present with:

- Excess body weight
- Poor breathing mechanics
- Poor abdominal tone
- Signs of poor digestion
- Weakness of the spinal muscles
- Poor posture

Organs Talk To Muscles and Joints

Every organ in your body has a muscle it's connected to by a nerve or series of nerves.

A problem or imbalance with an organ can lead to this imbalance being shared out across the corresponding muscles. For example, your kidneys talk to the muscles of the lower back.

These imbalances also affect the corresponding joints, for example the sacroiliac joint where your spine meets the pelvis, (at the waist band level of your trousers.) Therefore when looking for the root cause of your lower back pain, or any pain, it's worth bearing in mind that organ health is essential to long term joint health and muscles balance.

The digestive organs are linked to the abdominal muscles, sharing many nerve pathways. The abdominal muscles form an essential support network for your spine with connections directly to the lumbar spine, through areas of connective tissues.

If your abdominal muscles become weak or lose tone the functional relationship with your spine is poor, leaving your back open to excess wear and tear, because of poor posture during movement, for example.

Would you have thought that what you're eating is directly affecting the joints and disks of your spine?

Each of your organs also has associated emotions. Underlying fear for example, can be (but is not always) associated with lower back pain because of the connection of the kidneys and bladder with your lower back and their association with these emotions.

Fear and worry about money, relationships or job security can be mental and behavioural patterns that were perceived during your childhood unconsciously, that are now reflected outwardly into your life today, still waiting to be acknowledged and reconciled.

The past isn't dead, along with events that happened in your past, because time is an illusionary state.

The past isn't even past and the wounded parts of your mind may well be projected out onto your outer world, through body pain, to find the acknowledgment. This way your past lives on in the present!

Sitting Isn't Helping You

When it comes to the health of your spine, sitting on sofas and at a desk all day looking at computers is quite possibly one of the worst things you could be doing.

Your spine was not designed for slouching on a sofa unfortunately, even though it can feel quite comfortable at the time. It can take about three minutes to stretch the ligaments of the body, so anytime you sit with poor posture on the sofa with your lower back flexed and your upper back hunched over, you're stretching the ligaments into that position.

What's more, when you sit like that for a long period of time, in the evenings after work, watching television, for example, a few stretches every now and again in the gym just can't compete.

Once you've stretched excessive length into the ligaments of the lower back, you require the muscles and nerves to take over and provide a greater degree of support.

For healthy joints you require three elements; 1) the nerves, 2) the ligaments and 3) the muscles. If you lose the function of one you require the other two to pick up the slack.

Sitting at work with poor posture doesn't help either. A poorly designed chair, screen at the wrong height and inadequate lighting for your eyes will do wonders to exacerbate a flat lower back, hunched upper body and forward head posture. Is this you?

Even correct posture while sitting will cause muscle imbalances. Sitting badly causes excessive wear and tear on the disks and spinal structures. What's worse for your joints and muscle balance is sitting at work with poor posture all day then going to the gym.

Without a personalised programme that will help stretch the short and tight muscles of your body prior to exercising you increase the risk of injury.

Nutritional Nonsense

The world of diet and nutrition has gone mad. Are you confused by all the different approaches that seem to promise magical results?

An Amazon search for diet books can produce so many, with vastly differing ideas that you've no idea what is right or wrong. Should you do the raw vegan diet? Follow the Paleo diet? Atkins diet? Low GI diet? Super juicing diet? Blood type diet? 5:2 diet? Which approach will get the best results for you?

If you're confused about food, I'm not surprised. I think there's confusion amongst the experts who write these books and profess to have all the answers.

As many as 85% of people who have followed a diet and lost weight, regain the same weight or more within one year. Is this proof that weight-loss diets don't work? Is more exercise the answer to losing weight and maintaining a healthy physique?

What if more exercise is actually a drain on the resources

you're low on, due to lack of nutrients, poor hormonal health and toxicity? If you're trying to fill a bucket with water but there's a hole in the bottom, is it wise to turn the tap open more to get more water in?

What would you think if I said there are benefits in each of the nutritional philosophies? Would you believe there are potential drawbacks with them all as well? If just one book or philosophy had the answers you needed it might leave you blind to the fact that you are constantly in flux. Therefore if you follow one set of principles exclusively, the rigidity of your thinking may well take you out of balance eventually.

I'd like to share with you, one of the most powerful questions to consider when attempting to change your nutritional habits for the better:

What are the best foods to balance my body at this time?

This could result in you answering differently, on different days, at different times of the day and at different times of the year.

The only thing that never changes about the body is that it's always changing! You are constantly in a state of flux and your nutritional needs and supplementation that bring balance today are potentially going to throw you out of balance and move you away from optimal health tomorrow.

Fresh Juices

Fresh juices can offer you many benefits. They deliver a vast amount of easily digestible nutrients. You can potentially consume more vegetables and a wider variety in one sitting than you would do ordinarily. What's more, they can taste fantastic!

However what are you missing by doing juice cleanses and juicing diets? What are the hidden imbalances in your digestive system if you rely on them to remain in a healthy condition?

For example, you get acid indigestion and a colleague mentions that they benefited from doing a juice cleanse to get rid of their indigestion. You try it and it seems to work for you in the short term. After a few weeks of returning to solid foods and your regular diet you intermittently get the reflux again.

Do you need to stay on a juice diet? Or could you look at the proportion of fats, proteins and carbohydrates that you eat with each meal to provide a more favourable balance? What about the levels of hydrochloric acid (HCl) in the gut?

Paradoxically acid reflux can mean insufficient amounts of HCl. If you rectified the acid levels would that give you a more favourable outcome, plus help you absorb more nutrients, from a wider spectrum, that are available in proteins, fats and carbohydrates, as opposed to just vegetable juice?

Leading Causes of Death

In the UK the five leading causes of death are:

- Heart Disease
- Stroke
- Cancer
- Diabetes
- Accidents

Are you surprised by this list? Perhaps not. However, what do they have in common?

Diseases typically take 15-20 years to develop so if you know what to look for and how to make modifications in your diet, lifestyle and movement then you arguably have plenty of time to rectify an imbalance.

Epigenetics, in simple terms, is the study of how your lifestyle affects your genes.

Bruce Lipton found, in his work on the human genome project, that the 'environment' was responsible for approximately 90% of how a cell behaved.

For your body, the environment, which makes up the swimming pool within which your cells swim is linked to your diet, lifestyle and movement habits.

The five most common problems observed through client assessment that contribute towards secondary imbalances in your health, ultimately leading to the disease states mentioned are:

- Breathing Pattern Disorders
- Fatigue
- Food Allergies and Intolerances
- Imbalances In Gut Bacteria
- Blood Sugar Problems

These conditions are the body's way of communicating a message to you the best way it knows how. If you don't listen, the message will get louder and louder until a disease state occurs. These five symptoms are the states that precede the disease states of cancer, heart disease, diabetes and strokes either directly or indirectly.

Here's an example how a food intolerance could theoretically develop into something more serious over an extended time period.

You eat a couple of pieces of toast with butter and jam for breakfast as you have for as long as you can remember. The bread contains gluten and you have a mild intolerance. It's been that way for many years so the symptoms of slight bloating and a bit of gas don't even register for you. What's more, you're so busy you're not tuned into what your body's telling you. You get on with your day.

The slight bloating has, over time, caused your abdominal muscles to become weaker because of their connection to the small and large intestines, affected by the gluten in your diet. The disruption inside has resulted in a slight distention of your abdomen making it look like a little pot belly even though you're not really over weight.

The weakened abdominal muscles mean that your internal organs are now no longer held up where they should be, which is seen by the pot belly look (the weight of the organs falling forwards). They begin to fall forwards unchecked by the weaker abs. This abs/organ relationship means the large breathing muscle called the diaphragm is no longer tensioned, as it should be. Ultimately this affects how you breathe.

You may not be aware of any of these seemingly minor changes, so the cycle continues. You do, however, go and see a personal trainer to see what you can do about losing the belly and getting your abs back in some kind of shape. You get put on a fitness programme and the crunches and push ups contribute to make the existing muscle imbalances worse.

The muscle imbalances and disruption to the digestive system, albeit minor, cause your breathing pattern to change from a normal 'belly breathing' pattern to more of a chest pattern, where your chest rises and falls increasingly.

A chest breathing pattern uses more neck muscles and affects the nervous system. As a consequence a low level fight/flight response becomes hyperactive 24/7.

A constant, background fight/flight response is tiring on the body and you start to notice a level of fatigue you just can't seem to shake off no matter how much rest you get.

You're constantly fatigued and begin to consume more sugar or caffeine than you know is ideal but you just crave it and need a regular hit to keep going.

You start to gain weight and exercise becomes increasingly less effective to shift the extra pounds around the middle, what's more you begin to pick up niggling little injuries.

Eventually after months or even years of elevated blood sugar (due to the increased sugar and caffeine consumption) you develop diabetes diagnosed by the doctor and you get medication to help deal with your blood sugar.

While you're seeing the doctor you also ask her to have a look at your neck, which is becoming increasingly painful from time to time. The doctor then refers you for a course of physiotherapy on your neck.

The physiotherapist has limited time so you get treatment on your neck but he hasn't noticed your breathing pattern and what might be causing the problem. You then have repeated visits to the physiotherapist each time your neck plays up!

While that might not be the case for you and you don't have neck pain, I hope you can see how the journey from a lifestyle related imbalance can have far reaching effects.

The symptoms you present with months or years after the original complaint might be the tip of the ice berg. It could take careful assessment and time to ensure your lifestyle, diet and movement are balancing your body and contributing to your health and wellbeing instead of adding to the "stealth stress" that eludes the radar.

Beyond Symptoms

You might think that a holistic, whole body approach to health, fitness and wellbeing makes sense; to integrate all the parts of the body so they all sing in tune.

I'd certainly agree, it's what I teach clients day in day out but it's not how we, as a society, seem to approach health. I don't believe that imbalance is necessarily our fault but I do believe we can do something about it.

In Part 2, I'll show you how to gain peak performance in mind and body and live a brilliant life beyond self sabotage, find freedom from confusion about which foods are good or bad for you and how you can establish a relationship with food as a source of nourishment as opposed to torment.

You'll see the importance of posture and how to build postural correction into your daily habits. Learn about the foundations of movement and how to build a strong, healthy physique based on nature's design.

Finally see how you can keep yourself in tune once you have established an optimal level.

Part 2

The Steps To Getting
Back To Brilliant

The Steps

The steps to getting back to that optimal state of mind and body outlined in the introduction are laid out here in a five step method.

This is the method I employ with all private clients, which has worked remarkably well in helping a variety of health and fitness challenges over the last 10 years, including complaints such as long term back pain, poor sex drive, low energy, poor concentration, low self esteem, excess body weight and even clients on medication they no longer needed to take.

They are based on a collection of personal insights, advice from mentors and the teachings of Paul Chek, the founder of the *Chek Institute (USA)*, world leaders in holistic health and corrective exercise.

This method is a comprehensive, fully integrated approach to health and fitness.

I'm not going to show you how to get a six pack in six weeks or bulging biceps with two 'crazy' new moves. I won't be giving you advice on how to think positively or bestowing positive mantras to repeat to yourself each morning.

I believe that if you respect the laws of Mother Nature, you can have the washboard abdomen and the peace of mind without sacrificing other areas of your life. When there's harmony inside there will be harmony outside; true beauty.

Chaos breeds dis-ease and difficultly through unnecessary heat in the form of friction. Let's leave that behind and discover peak performance in mind and body - more energy, more peace of mind and a better physique.

To achieve that I have created the *5 R Method*.

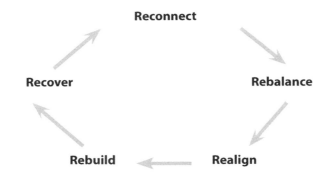

- *Reconnect* - Move beyond self sabotage and get to the know the real you
- *Rebalance* - Harness powerful relationships with food, sleep and breathing
- *Realign* - Perfect your posture as nature intended
- *Rebuild* - Build a strong and healthy body that looks great
- *Recover* - Strategies for maintaining your equilibrium

Back To Brilliant
Step 1: Reconnect

Reconnect is the first step, however it's an on going process of self awareness throughout your life. To reconnect is to uncover your most authentic self and achieve a sense of inner peace, a kind of harmony that allows you to flow gracefully through your life with less tension.

Before I delude you into thinking that following these steps makes life a walk in the park, it doesn't, but embracing your most authentic self allows more energy to flow into the right areas.

Wasting energy fighting the flow of the tide isn't the best way to experience life in my opinion. I'm pretty sure you've tried that. Surely there is more of a symbiotic relationship to be found.

In Part 1 you read about self sabotage and how that influences your health and wellbeing goals. Now I'd like to show you the different parts of the mind that are involved in some of your decisions, why you make them and how you can change your patterns of behaviour to your benefit for future success.

Anatomy of the Mind

The parts of the mind that make up the whole are comparable to your organs. Just like each organ has its own function, it operates most effectively as part of a system with other organs within your body.

Within each organ there are cells that makes up that organ. Each cell has important functions and when they work together the function of the organ is most effective. This could be equivalent to a part of your mind within a larger part, for example, your seven year old self within the child mind part.

What happens to an organ if cells begin to function independently of the other cells within that organ?

It's known as a disease.

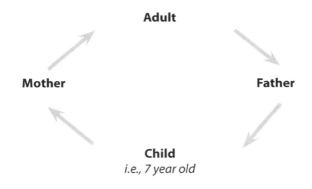

Each mind part has parts within it made up of experiences throughout your life, as you perceived them. Much like the organ in a disease state, when mind parts within other mind parts are conflicted we can become stuck in life, sabotaging any attempts to change.

Think back to the client story from Part 1; conflicted parts of his mind stopped him dead in his tracks, despite his best efforts to change.

The parts of your mind that behave as separate from the whole due to conflict can benefit from nurturing and acknowledgement.

The dis-ease between these parts of your mind can then be transformed into harmony and deeper levels of inner peace. And that might allow a smoother journey to achieving your goals.

Attributes of the Adult Mind
- Resists change therefore craves familiarity
- Has the capacity for critical thinking

Attributes of the Mothering Mind
- Is programmed by early childhood experiences
- Provides nurturing

Attributes of the Fathering Mind
- Is programmed by early childhood experiences
- Provides validation

Attributes of the Child Mind
- Naive, childish and needy
- Playful, childlike and creative

Control

Could your goals be an attempt to bridge a gap between who you think you are and who you wish you were? Where does who you actually are fit into this mix in respect of your goals? Your goals may be an attempt to experience a level of validation to a part of you that perceives it's missing or doesn't have enough. To the ego that craves the comfort of familiarity, changing the status quo could be perceived as a threat to its control.

Your mind likes to know what to expect. If it can predict the outcome of what might happen for each event in your life, it will feel in control. However, there's an issue with such an approach to life; growth and development will be stunted. New levels of self then can't be experienced through your goals. New equals different and different equals out of control to the mind, so new is shut down, thus new goals are not achieved.

To avoid the feeling of panic that comes from being out of control there are commonly five archetypes used to regain a sense of control, disguising the minds perceived threat.

These five archetypes are:

The Prostitute   **The Punisher**

The Mind's Control Team

The Victim   **The Saboteur**

The Rescuer

There are many different archetypes in the collective unconscious, that is the unconscious mind of human beings as a whole. These are said to be some of the most common.

Lets take a look at the attributes of each of the team members the mind uses to establish a pseudo sense of control and how they may be played out through your successful or unsuccessful goal achievement.

Answering the questions from JP Sears's *Living Beyond Self Sabotage* workshop might highlight aspects of each archetype.

Uncovering Your Inner Victim

- *The Victim* gains attention and acknowledgment through its own *pathetic*-ness
- Actively the *Victim* will blame others for not achieving its goals
- Passively the *Victim* blames self for not achieving its goals
- Paradoxically the more powerless the *Victim* becomes the more powerful it feels

1. Write down at least one experience that you can recall when you expressed either inwardly or outwardly the qualities of the *Victim*.
2. How would you imagine adopting the *Victim* archetype saved you from experiencing some amount of pain?
3. How would you imagine adopting the *Victim* archetype caused you some amount of pain?
4. How would you guess you experienced your mother expressing these attributes in your childhood?
5. How would you guess you experienced your father expressing these attributes in your childhood?

Uncovering Your Inner Rescuer

- The Rescuer gains validation through arrogance
- The inner *Rescuer* strives to find a sense of *being enough* but always finds it produces a sense of *not being enough*
- *The Rescuer* archetype appears in order to bring balance when a *Victim* is present or was present in childhood

1. Write down at least one experience that you can recall when you expressed either inwardly or outwardly the qualities of the *Rescuer*.

2. How would you imagine adopting the *Rescuer* archetype saved you from experiencing some amount of pain?

3. How would you imagine adopting the *Rescuer* archetype caused you some amount of pain?

4. How would you guess you experienced your mother expressing these attributes in your childhood?

5. How would you guess you experienced your father expressing these attributes in your childhood?

Uncovering Your Inner Punisher

*   The inner *Punisher* assumes power for itself by having power over another

*   The *Punisher* archetype brings attention to those with a void of attention in order to establish an equilibrium

*   The *Punisher* expresses outwardly what its inner reality actually is

1. Write down at least one experience that you can recall when you expressed either inwardly or outwardly the qualities of the *Punisher*.

2. How would you imagine adopting the *Punisher* archetype saved you from experiencing some amount of pain?

3. How would you imagine adopting the *Punisher* archetype caused you some amount of pain?

4. How would you guess you experienced your mother expressing these attributes in your childhood?

5. How would you guess you experienced your father expressing these attributes in your childhood?

Uncovering Your Inner Prostitute

- *The Prostitute* archetype gives up aspects of itself in order to complete itself and seduces itself and others resulting in a sense of betrayal
- Children who parent a parent are an example of the *Prostitute*

1. Write down at least one experience that you can recall when you expressed either inwardly or outwardly the qualities of the *Prostitute.*
2. How would you imagine adopting the *Prostitute* archetype saved you from experiencing some amount of pain?
3. How would you imagine adopting the *Prostitute* archetype caused you some amount of pain?
4. How would you guess you experienced your mother expressing these attributes in your childhood?
5. How would you guess you experienced your father expressing these attributes in your childhood?

Uncovering Your Inner Saboteur

- *The Saboteur* finds a level of gratification through the destruction of itself
- Modus Operandi: "The worse I become the better I am"
- May have its foundations in any of the other archetypes
- The principle motivation is the ego's fear of the power of true self

1. Write down at least one experience that you can recall when you expressed either inwardly or outwardly the qualities of the *Saboteur.*

2. How would you imagine adopting the *Saboteur* archetype saved you from experiencing some amount of pain?
3. How would you imagine adopting the *Saboteur* archetype caused you some amount of pain?
4. How would you guess you experienced your mother expressing these attributes in your childhood?
5. How would you guess you experienced your father expressing these attributes in your childhood?

By exploring the exercises above you open yourself to new levels of awareness about your habits, patterns and potential roadblocks to success.

While it can be uncomfortable to shine a torch light onto these potential blind spots, when you know you have a wound, it's much easier to help it heal than not knowing it's there and metaphorically bleeding to death.

If you've not found the wound, this usually results in discontinued efforts at changing something, be that, body weight, finances or relationships.

SUCCESS Goal Setting

SUCCESS goals are goals that allow you to embrace your most authentic self, negotiating the friction caused by sabotaged efforts of the past. They can assist in uncovering fertile soils in which growth and development can take place inwardly while achieving goals.

By considering both the light side of your goals, what you knowingly expect, and the shadow side, what a subconscious part of you expects, you're less likely to naively step out on the road toward your goal. Only considering the light side of the goal, you may become seduced by the known expectations, while a subconscious part craves the familiarity that comes with the status quo.

If 95% of people setting goals in the health and fitness industry fail to achieve what they desire, a new approach is surely needed. Looking at our inner Saboteur we can consider whether wounded ego parts are merely projecting our inner inadequacies outward onto our external world through the guise of goals. Traditionally you might focus on what you want to achieve, set priorities on what needs to be done to get there and then start taking action upon the path towards the goal.

What might not work with this method? What does a logical approach to goals miss that frequently ends in failure?

If you look at the parts of your consciousness that are less well know to you, through the SUCCESS goal setting process you open yourself to higher levels of awareness and less chance of being tripped up on your journey to goal attainment. How might you open yourself to higher levels of consciousness?

Lets take a look at each step of the SUCCESS goal setting method to do this:

S	Specific goal
U	Understanding what that means to you
C	Consequences (positive)
C	Consequences (negative)
E	Expectations of the goal
S	Sacrifice
S	Strategy

Specific Goal

Your specific goal gives a potentially abstract picture in your mind some boundaries and colour, with which you can begin to visualise it more clearly in reality. Your vision may contain the 'who, what or where and when' of your goal? For example, "My goal is to lose 5% body fat by 31st December and feel more energetic each morning."

Understanding What That Means To You

Looking at what your goal means to you helps you see the story beneath the story. This more complete picture moves you from the literal statement of your goal to a more symbolic representation, bringing colour, texture and shape to an otherwise two dimensional picture.

This can potentially bring a much deeper penetration into the psyche enabling you to connect with the root desires of your goal that are potentially not spoken outwardly through the words of your goal.

So you can ask yourself, "What does this goal mean to me?"

For example, "What would it mean to me to lose 5% body fat and have more energy?" To which you might reply, "I'd feel better about myself and feel more me!" Asking the question ,"What does that mean to me?" again allows another layer to be penetrated, to which you might reply, "It would be less effort everyday and I would feel like I was flowing with not fighting life."

At this point I hope you can see that we have only potentially gone two layers deep, however by moving into the symbolic landscape you are uncovering much more fertile soils in which you can sow the seeds of your goal.

With a skilled coach there may be benefit to exploring deeper layers, uncovering previously unexplored territory, going three, four or more layers deep to get to the epicentre of the desire for the rewards the goal will give.

Positive Consequences

Here you explore the benefits of your answers. This helps you to see a clearer picture of the known expectations for your goal. For example, what would you guess the benefits are of spending less energy everyday and flowing with life as opposed to fighting it?

You might say, "I'd have more energy for other things in my life. Without resisting what is already in my life, it would feel easier." or simply "I'd be happier."

Negative Consequences

If your conscious awareness is about 8% of your total consciousness, that leaves 92% that resides in the dark; your subconscious. By looking at the potential downside to your stated goal you might uncover some unexpected booby trap you would stumble into, had you naively gone about your goal without considering them.

Could missing this step alone result in sabotage for your goal? What could you guess might be the downside of life feeling like it's less effort everyday and feeling like you are going with the flow?

At first it sounds like an odd question to ask but it carries, potentially, an untold amount of power if you can accept that there may be a downside to your goal, for part of you.

Using our example, you might guess a downside to be, "I wouldn't know what to do with myself, it would feel so alien to feel like that." Importantly at this point, remember what we said was one of the attributes of the ego; familiarity; it craves familiarity! Therefore if achieving your goal would feel strange or unfamiliar your ego may fight that, because it sees that as a threat to its current control.

Expectations

Have you ever set a goal that felt so big, so far out in the distance that it seemed like it was unachievable? In fact many traditional approaches to goal setting say: "If it doesn't scare you its not a worthy goal".

A huge goal may feel incredibly gratifying at the time, to the ego certainly, but may crush your more authentic self under the weight of expectation. In fact how many times have you set goals, would you guess, that have been about ego gratification and not about becoming the best version of yourself? How did those goals turn out for you? Remember the ego seeks pleasure to avoid pain. Aren't these types of goals like building a house on quick sand?

Remember that creativity and playfulness are qualities that help embrace change so feeling overwhelmed by your goal is a way of stunting your creativity. How much expectation did you put on yourself to have fun when you played as a child? Didn't you just have fun, without thinking about it?

The more expectation you place on your goal, the more weight is resting on your shoulders.

How easy would it be to move around each day if you had to carry an extra 50kg on your shoulders?

Key question: How much expectation do I place on my goal on a scale of 1-10?

1   I'm not fussed either way.
5   I'll allow my goal to take shape as it feels right
        to do so.
10   I have to make this goal work!

Have you ever seen an 'underdog' sports team at the beginning of a season play with freedom, enjoyment and creativity. It all seemed so easy and they had smiles on their faces.

But as the weeks pass, because they'd been doing well not thinking about the results, the expectations started to rise and the creativity and free-flowing play began to look more stop-start and frustrated. The manager, who was carefree at the beginning of the season, now bemoans decisions his team made at critical moments in the game and makes excuses for their drop in performance.

What's changed?

The players are the same. The game is the same. The rules haven't changed. Yet the level of unspoken expectation has risen and stifled the creative, free-flowing fun that was a hallmark of the early weeks of the season.

When the expectation is a 10/10 it may just make the working conditions untenable to create the outcome that you're looking for. Can you make the ten a five? Read on to find out.

Sacrifice

If you feel that you really have to make your goal work, you might just be able to make it happen, if you work at it really hard. But, at the expense of what? Is that approach a sustainable way to live? Will it be an enjoyable path to reaching your goal or a grueling struggle?

What could you sacrifice about the goal to place less weight on your shoulders? In our example, could you extend the date by which you hope to lose the 5kg? Or could you get rid of an end date altogether? Could you set a goal to only lose 1kg to start with? How does the expectation feel now?

It really is a burden to carry a huge goal that feels too heavy. In contrast there can be nothing more invigorating than making small, continuous steps to a larger goal, each building confidence and enjoyment along the way. What might you need to sacrifice with your goal?

If you feel you can allow your goal to take shape when and how it feels right, then you will find you have a manageable, sustainable approach to your goal. Enjoy the process!

Strategy

The things you need to do and milestones you need to pass to achieve your goal is the final stage to consider. You may find that making a list of everything you think needs to be done, then prioritising that list a useful activity. Working through the list takes you step by step towards the goal.

Along the way, there are bound to be difficulties and resistance so it requires motivation and feedback along the way. Keeping a journal of how you feel about your journey as you go can be beneficial, for one, it gives you some time and space to process the thoughts and feelings you experience that may not always be consciously processed otherwise.

In Part 3 I'll give you a tool for this strategy section to keep track of progress and build feel good hormones so compliance and motivation both stay high.

Back To Brilliant
Step 2: Rebalance

Going Beyond Nutritional Non-sense

The world of diet and nutrition has gone mad in my opinion. Have you ever felt lost, confused or frustrated with the vast array of conflicting advice on diets? How can there be so much confusion about something that is such a primal necessity?

All you have to do is type 'diet books' into Amazon and you find a list as long as your arm and all with differing, mostly conflicting advice. For example, should you be a raw vegan? Follow the Paleo diet? Atkins diet? Low GI diet? Super juicing diet?

One week the 5:2 diet is all the rage and the next it's the high fat diet and cookbook that are portrayed as the missing link. Each time new diet or eating philosophy promises the answers to all mankind's problems!

As you've read, the ego likes to have control and having an answer, a precise answer, may be one way for the ego to feel in control.

Becoming overwhelmed by the vast array of opinions on nutrition and giving up caring represents the opposite end of the scale.

Let's assume that those two points of view are on a spectrum.

*I'm confused about
what to eat so I've
given up caring*

*I know exactly
what is best
for me to eat*

What would the middle ground be? What if it was something like, "I eat what feels best for me but sometimes I eat what I like"?

You could call this the 80/20 rule of diet; 80% of the time you eat to nourish your body and 20% of the time, you eat what you like and the result leaves you healthy, nourished and not needing to control food. How would you know if you've lost that 80/20 balance?

The results are dependent on what you want to achieve. If your aim is to be healthy and happy, there maybe more slack for you than someone who wants to optimise their body for sports or athletic performance. The point being, your approach is individual to you.

Orthorexia

Orthorexia is a term increasingly used to describe someone who is obsessed by health foods and eating 'perfectly'. People with this condition consider it a failure, or weakness to eat something not on a superfood list, containing an abundance of phytonutrients.

Again, the orthorexic person may be someone who says: "I know exactly what is best for me to eat".

However on our spectrum of extremes, the two ends are actually displaying symptoms of the same imbalance, simply expressed in a different manner, one as passive behaviour and the other as active behaviour.

What do both ends of the spectrum have in common?

They both use foods to deal with feelings they are not sure how to feel in other ways? These repressed feelings are simply projected onto the food.

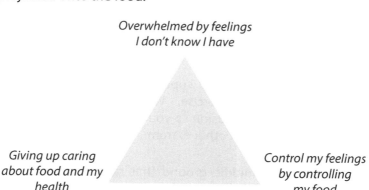

Overwhelmed by feelings
I don't know I have

Giving up caring
about food and my
health

Control my feelings
by controlling
my food

The diagram is an example of how you might feel from time to time with food. It might sound like this: all is perfect and you're eating really well, managing what you eat and feeling good then, a slip up or peer pressure in the office when the birthday cake's going round and 'that's it!' You might say to yourself, "I may as well have take away for dinner because it's been a bad day anyway" or, "Give me another piece of cake the days blown now".

This oscillation between, perfect eating and imperfect eating is rooted in deep emotional ground. The inner dialogue: "If it's not perfect I might as well start again tomorrow, and I will be perfect from then on" is a good example.

Except there's always a slip up, a bad day or those pesky office birthdays with cake and chocolate, that keep getting in the way of your perfect diet.

Superhuman orthorexia goals would aim "to be good from now on" implying you won't be 'bad' again ever! Yet you will. Why? Because humans are flawed and make mistakes.

To appreciate our fallibility is a healthy sense of shame as opposed to a toxic sense of shame displayed by the super-human type behaviour.

To not make mistakes, or try not to, is toxically shaming to yourself. What happens, you do end up making a mistake, be that with food or in life in general because you're human and that is okay. To think you won't ever make mistakes only reinforces the core toxic emotion you were running away from, perhaps unknowingly. 'Drop a waist size' fad diets reinforce this toxic shame in many of us.

Aiming to be perfect and superhuman sets up an elusive target with food and exercise. While being apathetic and overwhelmed with confusion so you don't even bother trying to make a change is the other extreme. What might the middle ground look like?

How about the middle ground that says, "I drink alcohol but I have healthy limits and know how much works for me?" Or even, "I eat chocolate but I prefer to have good quality, high cacao, organic sources when possible for a bit of a treat."

It's not saying, "I never eat chocolate because it's high in sugar and I can't do that on this health regime" or on the other end of the spectrum, "Sod it give me a Mars bar and Dunkin Doughnut too!"

The question then becomes, how do you develop a healthy relationship with food and feelings? And what might you be hiding from in acting superhuman and being perfect with your nutrition?

FEEDS

Using the *FEEDS* principles in a diary can help you to tune into what is happening for you when you're trying to make changes in the way you eat to improve health and vitality. FEEDS stands for:

F   Food and Fluids
E   Energy
E   Emotions
D   Digestion
S   Sleep

Food and Fluids

The category 'Food and Fluid' records what you've had to eat and drink on that day; anything that has passed your lips.

Does your meal leave you with a sense of satisfaction or cravings for something else? Do you feel satisfied after eating? Or do you generally feel stuffed?

Does your body tell you that what you're eating is working well for you or causing negative side effects? Do you even notice how food affects you?

Are afternoons a bad time for your energy levels? Do you tend to run hot or are you someone who is always cold (compared to those around you)?

Energy

The category looks at your energy levels following a meal? What do you notice about your energy immediately after your meal? Do you crash after a period of time following the meal? How long before you feel you need to eat again?

Emotions

How do your meals affect your emotional health? Do you feel stressed? Are you able to handle stress without it getting on top of you?

Do you notice an inability to think clearly and concentrate? Do you get easily agitated? Do you become depressed? Or are you manic?

Does thinking about food sometimes overwhelm you and you find it difficult to make decisions about what to eat?

Digestion

Your digestive health will help give you clues about what's happening on the inside. Basic observations about how often and how much fecal matter you pass each day is useful.

Are there partially digested food particles in your bowel movement? Is it foul smelling? Are your bowel movements consistent in shape and size? Do you have bowel movements every day or not very often?

Sleep

Your diet is incredibly important in respect of your sleep. If you eat according to what your body requires, it will manufacture the appropriate hormones. Sleep hormones are part of a group of hormones that are secondary to the fight/flight hormones.

If you are not eating the raw materials to make sleep hormones, your sleep will likely be poor. Fight/flight hormones take precedence as they keep you alive!

If you wake during the night, unrested or feel like you need a lot more than eight hours to feel rested there is a possibility you are not nourishing your body sufficiently.

10 Key Principles To Get You Started

I have deliberately been vague with what to eat because I believe you'll benefit from developing a healthy relationship with food by figuring out what works best for you. However to give you some context consider these 10 principles:

1. **Eat whole foods.** If you can get it out of the ground, or it lives off the earth it's a whole food. If it comes in a packet it's probably a manufactured product with a marketing team behind it!

2. **Buy organic.** With increased nutrient content, less toxins and less harm for the environment organic foods are a wise choice, should your budget allow.

3. **Avoid gluten and gluten containing products.** Gluten, which is found in grains such as wheat, rye, barley and products made with these grains such as bread, pasta and cakes is very often the cause of inflammatory conditions of the intestines.
This inflammation inhibits the optimal function of the abdominal muscles due to their connection with the intestines. Lower back pain, gas, bad breath and poor abdominal tone are potential consequences of gluten consumption.

4. **Avoid the four *white devils*.** White flour, white sugar, pasteurised dairy and white, refined salt.
   (More details below).

5. **Eat in a relaxed state.** Eating at your desk, on the run or in a meeting doesn't count as being relaxed.
If you're in an agitated state blood will be pumped away from the digestive system and towards the extremities. Foods will then sit in the digestive system, carbohydrates ferment, proteins putrefy and you have just created an ideal environment for parasites and fungus to grow!

6. **Eat raw foods as part of your diet.** Eating as much raw food as your digestive system can handle is a good idea.

Raw means abundant enzymes, unharmed by the heat of cooking and also more fibrous matter for a healthy bowel.

7. **Eat according to your individual metabolic needs.** Your metabolic needs are the proportions of protein, fat and carbohydrate that are right for your body. Everyone is completely different and varies day to day. Listen to your body and don't be afraid to add a little more protein, fat or carbohydrate if your body needs it. *(More details below)*.

8. **Eat the colours of the rainbow.** Different coloured foods contain different enzymes and nutrients within them. By maximising the number of different colours not only does it make your meals look appetising but it gives you the health and vitality benefits too.

9. **Rotate your foods.** Avoid eating the same foods constantly as this can contribute to food intolerances and inflammatory conditions in your gut. Rotating your foods on a four day cycle works well. Whatever you eat on a Monday avoid that same food again until Friday.

10. **Drink water!** Find out your weight in kilograms and multiply it by 0.0333. This will give you the amount of water your body needs. Get a re-useable water bottle and carry it with you to easily keep hydrated. As an example someone who weighs 76 kilograms would need to drink 2.5 litres of water a day.

Protein, Carbohydrate and Fat

When using your FEEDS principles to become aware of how your diet is affecting you and whether it's working well for you, consider the amounts of proteins, fat and carbohydrate you're eating. The amounts you need will vary at different times of the year, different days of the week and possibly from meal to meal.

The table shows you some potential feedback your body might give when you've eaten too much of either protein/fat or carbohydrate with your meal.

Too Much Carbohydrate	Too Much Protein
Energy highs followed by an energy crash	Feel food is sitting heavy on your stomach
Not getting the sensation of being full until your stomach is bloated	Mentally sluggish
You've started to accumulate fat around the middle	Your sweat starts to smell strong
You wake up between 2-4am to go to the toilet	Feel full but still want to eat
Lower back pain!	Neck/Shoulder pain!

Dr Weston Price, a dentist from Chicago, spent seven years traveling around the world back in the 1930s.

He stayed with indigenous tribes of people who were untouched by what he called 'White Man's food.' These were the foods that he'd begun to see his patients eating more of and he wondered whether it was these new processed foods that were making his patients' dental and general health progressively worse, in comparison to when he began his practice. He had seen a noticeable decline in the health of the teeth and mouths of those people he worked with and wanted to see exactly why.

In the seven year study, what he consistently found was that there were no indigenous people who had healthy teeth, jaw bones and physical development that were vegetarians.

However there were differing ratios of carbohydrates, proteins and fats in the diets. He stayed with Swiss families cut off from other villages reliant on making their own foods from the natural resources available. There were families in Africa who lived traditional tribal lifestyles and families on the South Sea

Islands of Polynesia.

In the book *Nutrition and Physical Degeneration* he shows pictures comparing those eating their indigenous diets and those who had started to break away. The contrast is quite shocking and just goes to show, *You Really Are What You Eat*. Importantly it also showed that each individual has a unique set of needs and there is no right diet for all. The environment was a significant factor in what these indigenous people's genes had evolved to utilise efficiently.

Metabolic Typing Basics

According to William Walcott in his book, *The Metabolic Typing Diet* there are three broad categories that you may fit into with your metabolic requirements for nutrients:

- A protein type
- A carbohydrate type
- A mixed type

These broad categories give you a starting point from which you can start to fine tune your nutritional needs by using the FEEDS principles as mentioned earlier.

Protein Type

As the name suggests if you're a protein type you will respond more favourably to a diet higher in proteins and fat. You may naturally be drawn to the darker meats such as beef, chicken thigh as opposed to chicken breast or richer heavier deserts. If you crave salty foods and your energy drops if you skip a meal consider proportioning your meals like a protein type as below.

For each meal use serving sizes based on the size of your palm and your fist. One fist is a good measure of one serving of carbohydrate and one palm is a good indicator for one serving of protein.

Try a ratio of - 3 palms:1 fist.

Begin your fine tuning using the FEEDS idea and don't be afraid to move up and down the spectrum of the amounts of protein and carbohydrate you need. Your body will tell you if you get it slightly wrong, if you are listening.

You'll be unlikely to be static on the spectrum. When your exercise intensity goes up, you'll require more protein.

Protein Type

Protein   *Carbohydrate*

Carbohydrate Type

If you're a carbohydrate type you will respond more favourably to a diet higher in carbohydrates and lower in protein and fat.

Carbohydrate Type

Protein   *Carbohydrate*

You may naturally be drawn to the lighter meats such as chicken breast or white fish as opposed to fish such as salmon and mackerel that contain more fat or you may prefer lighter deserts.

Try a ratio of - 1 palm:1.5 fists.

Mixed Type

As the name suggests if you're a mixed type you will respond more favourably to a diet with more of a balance of proteins and carbohydrates. You may naturally be drawn to the darker meats at some times and lighter meats on other occasions.

Try a ratio of - 1 palm:1 fist

Mixed Type

Protein   Carbohydrate

Quick Exercise

You need a tape measure and a calculator.

Use the tape measure to measure the circumference around your waist at belly button level.

Now measure the circumference around your hips. (Find the bony bits of your pelvis that stick out roughly where your waist band might be on you trousers)

Divide the first number by the second number then multiply that by 100 to give you a percentage.

If your number is greater than 100% as a male and 80% as a female, you are showing an increased risk of any of the diseases outlined in Part 1 - cancer, heart disease, diabetes and strokes.

This test is indicating that blood sugar management is one of your key areas for improvement and metabolic typing is a good place to start.

The 4 White Devils

The four white devils are foods that Dr Weston Price found were commonly causing a problem in indigenous people throughout the world, in relation to their health and wellbeing. These 4 white foods are:

- White flour and products made from white flour
- White sugar
- White salt (refined table salt)
- Pasteurised dairy

If you consume these foods in your diet, or foods made with them, then you are likely to increase your risk of suffering health challenges.

These items are actually non-foods, meaning they take nutrition from the body while digesting them, they are empty calories. Your body can't use foods of such poor, refined quality as it needs the nutrition from proteins, vitamins and minerals to help metabolise them. Therefore if you eat them regularly you may be depleting stores of minerals from the body.

In the case of white, processed sugar, if you eat it without other nourishing foods containing quality vitamins and minerals the sugar is not digested and utilised fully.

Pyruvic acid builds up in the brain and nervous system and accumulates in the red blood cells affecting the respiration of the cell. Once this happens the cells can't get enough oxygen and ultimately cells will die.

Once cells start to die in a part of the body, functioning is affected and degenerative disease is likely to set in in the longer term. Remember in Part 1 we talked about the five most common killers in the UK being, cancer, heart disease, strokes, diabetes and accidents. Starvation of cells is how a stroke happens!

Minimising white sugar is a wise choice. Eliminating sugar completely can result in abundant health in the longer term.

Fat is Your Friend

Fat really is your friend but saturated fat may even be your best friend! Yes you did read this correctly I said saturated fats. The following is a list of why saturated fats should not be cut in your diet if you want to eat healthily and nourish your body.

- Your cell membranes need to be made of saturated fat for it to have sufficient stiffness and integrity. When the cell wall is deficient in saturated fat it can't work properly.
- Saturated fat protects the liver from toxins. So if you do go out and drink alcohol you are best to consume a meal high in saturated fat beforehand. Although the drinking is not part of the recommendations here!
- Saturated fat lowers Lp(a) which is a good predictor of heart disease.
- Saturated fat lowers C-Reactive proteins which are an indicator of inflammation, which many studies show is responsible for heart disease.
- Saturated fat, omega 3 fatty acids and cholesterol all work together to maintain normal kidney function which is critical for managing blood pressure and filtering toxins.

Cholesterol also gets a bad rap from many areas, or certainly has over the past 30 plus years. If you're concerned about your cholesterol levels rising if you increase your saturated fat intake, keep reading for some interesting information.

You should know at this point that levels of total cholesterol (HDL + LDL) are not accurate markers of heart disease.

In fact cases of heart disease are just as high in those with low cholesterol as they are with high cholesterol.

The benefits of cholesterol:

- Your body uses cholesterol to make vitamin D which is necessary for muscle growth, immune system function, bone health and proper function of the nervous system.
- Dietary cholesterol plays an important role in maintaining the health of the intestinal wall.
  This is why vegetarian diets can lead to digestive problems such as leaky gut syndrome.
- Your body needs cholesterol to make all sex hormones.
- All sleep and repair hormones are made from cholesterol.

There is one very important thing that supersedes this information on fat; that's source and processing. Source and processing rarely get considered when talking about saturated fat and cholesterol in respect of health. It's either 'fat is good or fat is bad.' This may or may not be the case though.

Here's an example of how source (where your meat comes from and how it's fed) and processing affects your health.

Animal fats can change depending on how the animal has been raised. If the beef that you eat has been grass-fed it will contain levels of conjugated linoleic acid (CLA), which has good anti-cancer properties, helps build muscles tissue and prevents weight gain. This acid however, disappears when cows are fed even small amounts of grain or processed feed!

So, buying the absolute best quality meat and vegetables you can afford and preparing food well are essential steps to maintaining a good level of health and protecting against heart disease, cancer and other major health challenges.

The order of preference might look something like:

1. *Soil Association* organic meats and vegetables
2. *Soil Association* organic meats but conventionally grown vegetables

3. Free range meats and *Soil Association* organic vegetables
4. Conventionally reared/grown meats and vegetables

Food Rotation

Food rotation can be an important step in reducing the chances of you acquiring a food intolerance. How does a food intolerance differ from an allergy though?

Food intolerance	Food allergy
Reactions can arise up to 72 hours after eating	Reactions are usually immediate
Many different foods can be involved	Rarely more than 1-2 foods involved
Involves immune antibody type IgG	Involves immune antibody type IgE
Symptoms can clear after avoidance of offending foods for a period of time	Lifelong immune response to allergic foods

Why should you choose to follow a food rotation diet?

Food intolerances are very easy to acquire by over eating a particular food group without rotating it, because the body uses up the enzymes responsible to breaking it down when you eat chicken all the time, for example. You may also have a leaky gut, which is where the intestinal wall allows food particles that aren't fully digested, to escape into the blood stream and then the immune system becomes sensitised to that food group and therefore sees it as an 'invader'.

Each subsequent meal with that food group will challenge the immune system, leading to reduced immune efficiency, fatigue, poor skin, weight gain, joint aches and pains, constipation and many other symptoms.

A leaky gut can be caused by many factors but some of the most common are; stress, consuming alcohol on an empty stomach and eating foods you are intolerant to.

The method of food rotating I recommend, which is easiest to follow is a 4 day food rotation. That means whatever you eat on the first day, Monday for example, you avoid until Friday.

A 4 day rotation might look like this:

	Day 1	Day 2	Day 3	Day 4
Breakfast	Scrambled egg with side salad	Leftovers from dinners	Tuna with rocket and red pepper salad	Leftovers from dinner
Lunch	Chicken breast, roasted sweet potato and fennel with avocado salad	Home-made lamb burger	Pork goulash with a serving of rice	Beef stew, steamed cavalo nero and broccoli
Dinner	Marinated chicken skewers, roasted aubergine and courgette	Lamb cutlets with roasted squash, red onion and corn-on-the-cob	Swedish meatballs (pork) with steamed broccoli, carrots and green beans	Steak, with asparagus and mange-tout

Making this a priority to change in your current diet is a great idea. I can't recommend it enough. The amount of health challenges that can come from food intolerances, needlessly, because you're over eating one or two foods and not adding variety into your diet are enormous.

Food allergy and food intolerances are factors in lower back pain, neck and shoulder pain for chronic sufferers who have had little or no results with traditional approaches. The food particles that get through a leaky gut and into the blood stream can, and do, get into the lining of the joint tissues of the body, and then the immune system will begin to attack those 'foreign' particles as they are seen as a threat by the immune system.

Due to the fact the invader is now forming part of the joint tissue, the whole joint can come under attack from the immune system as it can't distinguish between normal joint tissue and the invader that shouldn't be there. The immune system will think that the tissue needs disposing of to maintain the health of the organism so at begins its processes to erode the tissue. Unfortunately as the foreign particles form part of the joint tissue, they are attacked too and then start to become a problem as inflammation and pain at a joint.

This is an example of an auto-immune disease.

State Of Mind While Eating

Do you eat at your desk while catching up on emails? Do you eat while you're walking around, 'on the run'? Do you take phone calls during your lunch break?

When you're concentrating on work, moving around or being distracted while you're eating, such as, grabbing a bite of a sandwich while you're preparing for the next meeting it's not ideal for digestion. In these examples you're likely to be in heightened state of awareness, concentrating, which requires your brain to be in a beta brain wave state. Your blood will move from the digestive organs, where it needs to be and out into the muscles and generally towards the periphery, reducing the effectiveness of the digestive system.

The beta brain wave state is also associated with the fight/ flight stress state. In the fight/flight mode your body requires blood in the muscles to fight or run (flight). What happens to your sandwich or piece of fruit when the blood is out in the periphery?

The food will make its way down into the digestive system and then remain there moving along much more slowly.

Ideally digestion requires a calm, relaxed environment to do its best work. When foods sit in the digestive system longer than they should, carbohydrates begin to ferment in the nice warm and moist environment inside and proteins will putrefy.

Not a pleasant thought but it's a common scenario in today's busy world. Could this go some way towards explaining why 80% of the world's population is living with a fungal infection?

When stress is high, carbohydrates fermenting in your gut are an ideal meal for fungus and parasites. Even worse, you might notice you have a bad taste in your mouth from time to time and you can't work out why. Fermenting food in your gut may go some way to explaining this bad taste as well as your general aches and pains.

How do you create an ideal brain wave state for digestion?

Getting away from your desk is a good suggestion.

It's likely you associate your desk with productivity and being busy. So, if you are eating at your desk you are probably approaching eating as another task to get done.

Finding somewhere quiet, calm and relaxed to eat is ideal.

Switching off your mobile phone and not checking emails is also a good idea. Reading can be a problem for some people as the eyes take a lot of energy and can compromise effective digestion, but test how you get on. Reading something funny or relaxing can help you switch off for a few minutes from work.

Make appointments with yourself for lunch, honour those appointments like you would a meeting and give yourself some peace and quiet. Taste your food, chew every mouthful until liquefied and allow the digestive system to do its work.

If you really are feeling stressed, avoid eating at all until you can honestly say you feel relaxed and can enjoy the food. Otherwise the food isn't going to be utilised fully by the body, no matter how good the quality.

Slow Cooking

I highly recommend a slow cooker. Being busy with lots of responsibilities and demands on your time, work deadlines, social functions and client commitments might make it difficult to always have the time to start cooking meals when you get home at night during the week.

Using a slow cooker has been a saviour for me and I'm sure it can be for you as well. Even if you're not the main chef in your house and don't have to worry about time in the kitchen too much there are still benefits to cooking more slowly.

Remember I said that the source of your food and how it's processed were important factors? Let me explain about food processing.

As you now know fat is an essential part of your healthy diet, as long as you have invested wisely in preferably organic, free-range meats. However you can damage fats by cooking at high temperatures.

High heat processing of food, particularly fats can cause them to go rancid, produce free radical damage and convert the healthy fat into trans fats that damage your health instead of improve it.

Using the slow cooker, you'll be able to prepare a meal in 20 minutes, or less sometimes, have the food ready for you when you get back from work and have the healthy fats intact.

The temperature of the slow cooker means you are maintaining the health benefits of the fats in your food, not destroying them. One pot cooking also means less mess in the kitchen and that must be less stressful, so there are benefits all ways round.

Salting Your Water

Putting salt in your water maintains a good mineral content and supports optimal hydration. The concentration of salt in the water within your cells is greater than that of fresh drinking water so, if you start to drink lots of clean, fresh water you could actually draw salts from the body, particularly if the mineral content of the water you drink is low.

For every litre of water you drink if you add one pinch of good quality, sea salt that has not been processed or had anything added, such as anti-caking agents, you'll be doing wonders for your body.

If you find that you start drinking more water and you need to go to the toilet a lot, I've found that adding a pinch of salt to each litre can reduce frequent urination. Also, if you drink a lot of water yet you still feel dehydrated at the end of the day this too can be a signal that you are drinking low mineral water.

Drinking more and adding salt can also increase your energy so if you're finding that one of your primary problems is fatigue this is an easy first step.

A toxic body is likely to be a tired body, so how do you start to detoxify? An easy solution is hydrating well. If your body is polluted with toxins each of the detoxifying organs run, using water. Without adequate amounts of water for these processes there'll be a build up of toxins within each of these organs.

The best solution for pollution is dilution.
Robert Rakowski

Beware of tap water though, water reports show that many municipal sources of water are polluted with heavy metals and even recreational drugs. Tap water also contains chlorine, to kill some of the nasties, but chlorine also kills the friendly bacteria in the digestive system. Remember how important a good balance of bacteria is in the gut. It pays to drink quality water.

Using a whole house filtration system with a good quality water filter will help you have access to water that will support as opposed to detract from your health.

Timing Of Hydration

If you want to achieve the best from your body, detoxify, increase energy and improve digestion, hydrating adequately is an easy first step. I highly recommend you follow the advice given by Dr Fereydoon Batmanghelidj about the amount of water to consume each day.

Find your body weight in kilograms
x 0.0333 = Litres of water per day

You might think that's a lot of water for you to drink if you're only drinking about a glass or two at the moment. So how can you drink that much? A good strategy is to commit to drinking water before each meal.

Having a glass or two before each meal, (about 400ml) will allow your body to absorb and utilise the water to make hydrochloric acid which is used for digesting food in the stomach, one of the earlier stages of digestion. The strength of hydrochloric acid in your stomach and the amount is important. Poor digestion, poor absorption and acid indigestion are often symptoms of dehydration and therefore low acid levels in the gut.

I don't recommend that you drink during the meal and also leave about 20 minutes between drinking the water and starting your meal to allow your body to absorb the water.

Having a drink of water prior to your meals means you'll get about 1.2 litres of vital fluid by incorporating this new habit. Then the remainder of your daily quota can simply be sipped throughout the rest of the day.

If you fill your stomach with water while you're eating you can dilute the power of the acid and digestive processes making it less effective. And if you are sipping your water throughout the day in between meals you won't feel the need to drink lots with your meal. It is best if you leave 20-30 minutes after a meal before you drink any significant volume of water again for the benefit of digestion.

Post Workout Carbs

When you've become familiar with how your body reacts to different levels of carbohydrate, protein and fat at each meal you'll notice improvement in your health. You'll not have energy highs and lows, your concentration ability will improve and you'll start to respond more favourably to your efforts with your exercise programme.

After a workout your muscles will be depleted in glycogen (a stored form a sugar in the muscle), if you are eating correctly anyway. The timing for re-fueling yourself after a work out and what it consists of are important to maximise your efforts in the gym, build solid muscle and improve recovery, ready for your next exercise session.

The first 30 minutes following an exercise session your muscles are more receptive to replacing the glycogen you've used, therefore this is an ideal time to eat following your session. The further from the session you get, the less receptive to blood sugar the muscles are and the more chance high blood sugar levels will convert to fat and collect in unwanted places.

The good news is you can get away with more carbohydrates within 90 minutes of exercise. The healthy proportions of carbohydrate, fat and protein that are working well for you following the Metabolic Typing concept can be supplemented by an extra serving of a starchy carbohydrate such as rice or potatoes or fruit for desert.

This added sugar from the increase in carbohydrate will be converted into glycogen and stored in your muscles. This can give you more of an athletic appearance in the short term as the muscles look fuller because of the extra glycogen. However there is a limit to how much they can store and also how much the liver can store. Therefore it's important to listen to your body's needs for how much carbohydrate, protein and fat are working optimally for you. Eating too much carbohydrate to achieve this effect on the muscles will be counter productive if you over do it and begin accumulating fat around your abdomen.

Vitamin D Foods

Vitamin D is responsible for almost all chemical reactions in your body according to Dr Mercola from *www.mercola.com*.

In countries with a greater amount of sunlight it's easier to get your quota by being out in nature and soaking up Vitamin D from the sun via the skin.

Traditionally, those of us that live in the northern part of Europe have used high quality sources of food that supplies us with vitamin D.

Vitamin D has been shown to help protect against:

- Cancer
- Heart Disease
- Diabetes
- Obesity
- High blood pressure
- Chronic pain

I wrote about the pioneering work of Dr Weston A Price and his trips around the world to study indigenous people and their diets. He found that people with superior health, even those in areas with adequate exposure to sunlight, consumed foods high in vitamin D. This is why you would be wise to add high quality vitamin D from a food source to help protect you against disease and optimise your health.

The following foods are high in vitamin D:

- Fermented cod liver oil
- Organ meats - from organic, grass fed animals
- Wild caught salmon
- Eggs - from free range, organic chickens
- Unpasteurised butter - from organic, grass fed animals

As you age your ability to absorb vitamin D through the skin decreases significantly and by 70 years of age it has dropped four-fold. As well as ageing, working inside, wearing clothing that blocks the absorption of UV rays and city buildings that block direct light all affect your ability to absorb and utilise UVB rays from the sun.

Breathing

Breathing is clearly very important to health and ancient disciplines such as Yoga, Tai Chi and Qigong have placed breathing at the centre of their practices for hundreds of years. In fact Qigong literally translates into breath work.

Breathing exercises refill the body's natural stores of energy and even help to replenish them when depleted through periods of stress or disease.

A normal respiratory rate is about 12-16 breaths per minute, however with specific Qigong exercise you can take the breath down below 10 breaths per minute. This enables you to waste less energy and uptake increased levels of oxygen with greater efficiency.

According to Ken Cohen, a Qigong grandmaster and founder of the *Qigong Research and Practice Centre*, says the following qualities indicate healthy breathing:

Each breath should be:

- Deep
- Long
- Even
- Smooth
- Slow

More than 50% of the populations of the West have inverted or chest breathing patterns as opposed to belly or diaphragm breathing.

When the diaphragm is involved in breathing the lower lobes of the lungs become active and this is where most of the oxygen exchange takes place.

A chest-breathing pattern causes the body to become progressively more energy deficient.

Chest breathing also affects the following aspect of the body:

- Increases the Acid:Alkaline ratio (most people are too acidic already)
- Increases the breathing rate
- Decreases the levels of oxygen delivered to bodily tissues
- Constricts blood vessels
- Decreases circulatory function
- Increases energy starvation of the heart and brain
- Unsettles the mind increasing anxiety
- Causes chronic fatigue

What Breathing Should Look Like

Effective breathing starts from the belly and rises up into the chest and neck in the final third of the breath. Take a deep breath in. Does your belly come out for the first part of the breath? Does your abdomen inflate like you have a rounded belly? Or does your stomach go flat and your chest rises as you take a nice deep breath in?

If your stomach goes flat or inwards and your chest rises this is what's knows as an inverted or upside down breathing pattern. This will cause major bio-chemical problems in your body if you continue to breathe this way when you're not exercising or performing a physical movement.

Your whole physiology shifts when you breathe like this and you may well begin to develop symptoms such as headaches, neck pain, shoulder pain and back pain to name a few from such breathing. In fact it's so significant that any present or past symptom could potentially be traced back to an inverted breathing pattern.

When you breathe, if you do so with a big belly breath for the first 2/3rd it allows the diaphragm, the large respiratory muscles under your rib cage to move down into the abdominal organs (stomach, intestines, liver etc) and push them forwards, massaging them at the same time.

This also stretches the deep abdominal muscles and creates a tension in them. As you breathe out again the belly button should move back toward the spine and push the diaphragm up again and the deep abdominal muscles also hold the organs back in place.

The relationship between the breathing muscle, the diaphragm, and the deep abdominal muscles are essential for the health of your entire body.

Life and Death

Breathing is important! I think we can agree on that. It's so important in fact that the body will do just about anything it has to in an effort to maintain an airway and oxygenate itself.

As many as 12% of all hospital visits in the USA are due to breathing pattern disorders, that is not breathing naturally, creating a plethora of symptoms.

Things That Disrupt Breathing

In simple terms, anything can disrupt an optimal breathing pattern. Be aware of actions that disrupt your breathing pattern, which can cause health issues if left unaddressed.

What I mean is, if you perform an intense exercise session, a heavy weights session or maybe a cardiovascular session you'll be breathing using the same muscles I described in the upside down breathing pattern, that is, using the neck muscles as well as the diaphragm. However once you stop doing the activity that causes you to breathe more heavily, you should revert to belly breathing. If you are still breathing upside down there are some common causes such as:

- **Poorly designed exercises or programmes**
  Are improved aesthetics worth sacrificing your health
  and wellbeing?
  Is there any point in looking better on the outside,
  if you feel terrible in the inside? Does looking good
  and being healthy have to be exclusive of one another?
  In my opinion, no they don't. It does, however,
  mean exercise must be viewed slightly differently.
  Prior to performing an exercise or set of exercises,
  it makes sense to know what your body requires to gain
  balance and therefore achieve improved performance.
  Symmetry, afterall is beauty.
  While a full bio-mechanical screening for the length
  and tension of muscles prior to developing an exercise
  programme is not a regular practice, this can make
  the difference in how you look and feel in the long run.

- **Stop eating gluten.**
  All grain foods except, corn, rice, buckwheat and millet
  contain gluten. So your favourite breads, wraps,
  porridge oats, pasta and bagels can cause bloating
  and disrupt your functional abdominal breathing.
  Interestingly 60% of Caucasian people are gluten
  intolerant.

- **Become aware of your food intolerances.**
  You can be intolerant to any food. For example,
  I'm intolerant to grapes. This is unusual but you may
  well have strange food intolerances yourself
  that you don't know about.
  Most commonly the foods you eat regularly affect you.
  These are called acquired intolerances so look at
  your weekly food intake and be mindful of how you
  feel following each meal.

There may well be foods inflaming your stomach and digestive organs. Using the FEEDS principles is a useful tool to observe how food and fluids are affecting you.

- **Emotional stress affects your health.**
  If you feel like crying or getting angry do you let it out? Why? Where does that pent up energy go if its not expressed? There are possibly unexpressed tensions that are sitting in muscles and organs right now. Could some of this excess tension be sitting in the muscles of healthy respiration? That is, the diaphragm? In stopping yourself from expressing emotions, particularly around love and connection, you may be inhibiting the ability of your breathing muscles to work properly. Digestive and neck problems can be the consequence of such imbalances.

- **Poor posture can be related to a carelessly designed exercise programme.**
  More specifically however I mean ergonomics. How you position yourself in your environment on a daily basis. Do you sit well in the car? At your desk at work? On the sofa at home? Do you have good technique when you exercise? Let's not forget just standing up straight with good alignment. All these postural habits will inhibit your ability to breathe well particularly if you slump and therefore make it difficult to belly breathe fully. With good postural alignment and good ergonomics you'll stand a better chance of belly breathing properly and avoiding unnecessary side effects on your neck, shoulders and back.

- **Over consumption of sugar is not good for you.**
  Sugar is a very powerful stimulant even in small amounts. For example, a single teaspoon of sugar can suppress the immune system for up to six hours. Sugar can also cause an acidifying effect on the cells of the body. When this happens the body tries to balance itself by bringing in more alkaline. One of the fastest ways to do this is breathing in oxygen, therefore speeding up

the breathing rate. An increased breathing rate for the nervous system triggers a fight/flight response. The breathing at this point is likely to flip into the upside down pattern again.

Age and Breath

Do you look older than you think you should for your years? The ageing of every cell in your body speeds up when your breathing speeds up or is not as efficient as it could be.

You have three major systems that control the rhythms within the body, called biological oscillators. These three systems are the intestines, the heart and lungs and the brain. When the three are in sync and running well the body is in optimal health. However, when under pressure physically, mentally or emotionally they can be knocked out of rhythm. For example, have you ever felt so nervous you felt sick? What was your breathing like in that moment, slow and relaxed or short and quick?

When the biological oscillators are out of sync you'll experience a lack of optimal health, which will cause you to age more quickly than you would if all three systems were balanced. Practicing a breathing discipline like Tai Chi, Qigong or yoga promotes harmony of the brain, heart and lungs and intestines.

In Part 3, I give you a simple, daily Qigong exercise.

Quick Exercise

To test whether you are in fight/flight state and therefore creating some of the symptoms I've mentioned, such as altered blood pH, there is a simple test you can do by holding your breath.

Sit upright in a chair with a timer handy.

Take a breath in and hold your breath while starting the

timer simultaneously. How long can you comfortably hold your breath?

If you fail to make the 50 second mark you are likely to be in a fight/flight state and therefore the body needs to increase the breathing rate. You are likely too acidic and the body wants to get oxygen in to neutralise the pH.

If you make 50-75 seconds you are showing that your body's pH balance is likely to be in good shape.

The Why and When of Sleep

Sleep is essential to your health, but when you sleep is also important for long-term health and wellbeing. Sleep is driven by the influence of the sun and the moons cycles on your hormonal system. It's well known that you need eight hours restful sleep to fully recharge at night. However getting to sleep at midnight and sleeping until 8am is not as good for you as sleeping from 10pm and waking at 6am. But why?

You have cycles of repair that ideally happen at given times. Between 10pm and 2am your body goes through physical repair and heals all the micro traumas that occur throughout a normal day of living and being active. Then, from 2am until 6am the body goes through a psychological repair phase.

This is why, if you sleep badly or you are constantly waking during this period of the night, you can have memory challenges and decision making can become hard, even for the most simple of tasks.

The questions below may give you a pointer towards whether you're not getting adequate sleep quality in the 10pm - 2am period:

- Do your bones feel tender, sore and achy throughout your body?
- Do you suffer with lower/upper back pain?
- Is bending and stretching down to the floor in the morning difficult?

- Do you injure, strain or sprain easily or more easily than you used to?
- Do you feel unrefreshed upon awakening?

These questions will show whether you're not getting quality sleep in the 2am - 6am period:

- Are chunks of new information difficult to absorb?
- Are you forgetful?
- Is your tolerance for stress and life challenges low or lower than it used to be?
- Have you noticed you bump into things more frequently than you used to?
- Do you feel like you need extended sleep, like 10-12 hours, to feel human again?

Your Oldest Tonic

I honestly feel that quality sleep is the most primal tool in your health and wellbeing tool kit. After all, every single one of your blood cells is photosynthetic, meaning light from the sun will convert into usable energy.

This is the same system plants use to produce energy, which is ancient in evolutionary terms. If it were not important for humans to be photosynthetic our genetics would have adapted to no longer need the process. Darkness and light play a role in health.

Humans are so sensitive to light that a tiny spot of light on the back of your leg in a pitch black room would be enough to make your stress hormones rise. This is one argument for making sure your bedroom is pitch black, so you can fully rest each night.

If you are suffering with lower back pain, getting to bed earlier and making sure you sleep well for eight hours each night is a must.

Adrenal fatigue and burnout are quite commonly associated with lower back pain because this is where the nerves that communicate with the adrenal glands, are located. The adrenal glands pumps out the hormones responsible for keeping you awake.

The average number of hours of sleep we get today is less than our ancestors. Just 100 years ago people were averaging 11 hours a night. Without television and devices to keep stimulated our forebears were probably feeling drowsy earlier than we do in these digital times.

The light from the television or other devices such as iPads or mobile phones stimulate the pineal gland and affects the reticular activating system, the part of your brain responsible for registering arousal.

Your body thinks its midday when you're looking at the bright light of these electrical products and increases the activating hormones accordingly. Not so good if you're supposed to be winding down and relaxing after a busy day at work.

Leave your mobile devices out of the bedroom. The electromagnetic field and the light it emits are not helping you get a deep, restful night's sleep. Read more about the electromagnetic field and its influence on your body in the *Recover* section; the final step of the 5R's.

If you wake up and feel you're not refreshed and ready for a busy, productive day and would rather bury your head back in the sheets, I suspect that your stress hormones have been too high for too long the previous day. Your body might not have been in a relaxed state until midnight or 1am meaning you could have had as little as five hours restful sleep. This is a recipe for a cascade of health challenges and chronic physical aches and pains.

Sleep is the most regenerative force in the world.

Repair vs Trauma

You now understand that the body needs good, deep restful sleep to repair its systems; physically, psychologically and hormonally.

When this is not happening due to exposure to light, going to bed too late, drinking caffeinated drinks too late in the day or having a stressful environment at home, you may start to fall apart! Injuries and issues that are nagging away will not clear up, no matter whom you see for advice.

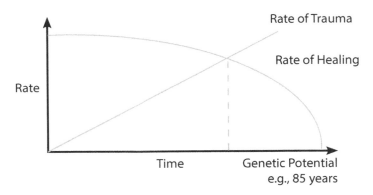

The first graph above shows that as you get older the rate at which your tissues repair themselves slows down very slightly until you get into your later years when the repair slows dramatically.

You can influence the rate at which your body repairs itself though, by getting good quality sleep, eating what your body requires and following a well designed exercise programme.

Keeping stress down and hydrating are also factors that maximise your genetic potential.

Being unaware or ignoring these aspects of health and wellbeing could decrease your rate of repair and increase the rate of cumulative trauma in your body.

Degeneration occurs quicker than if it were purely down to your genes.

Depending on what damage is happening and what tissues are being stressed, this aging process can lead to chronic injury, joint pain or premature death.

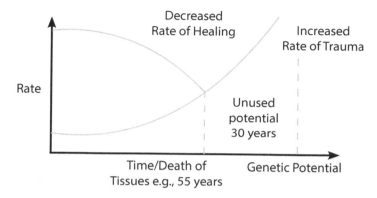

The diagram above shows the lines converging much quicker than they would do if it were purely down to your genes.

Depending on what damage is happening and what tissues are being stressed this can lead to chronic injury, pain in a joint or death as depicted!

Lighting

To prevent over stimulation and inhibiting the release of melatonin, the sleep hormone, at the correct times in the ideal amount, limiting your use of tablet, mobile, television and laptop after 8pm works well. These devices emit a strong, sun-like, bright light that tell your pineal gland it's the middle of the day, and trigger activating hormones.

Turning off bright lighting, using candles or dimmer switches to simulate dusk is an ideal scenario for the evening. If you can do this you will sleep much more deeply, I'm sure.

Client Story

I once worked with a woman who wanted to lose weight while also working on her posture and lower back pain.

I did a thorough assessment and suggested lifestyle changes that would help her body regain a balanced state to allow her to drop the excess weight.

When we came to re-measure and assess how well the plan had been working, we found only small changes, which were not proportionate to what we expected.

When reviewing her plan, we discussed her sleep habits and hit a problem. She was finding it difficult to change her routines and would often remain on the computer sending emails until after midnight. We spoke about how this habit would impede her results yet this logical approach was not getting through. She knew her late night computer work wasn't conducive to making strides to a healthier lifestyle yet she just couldn't make the change.

It wasn't until she went away camping in the summer that she finally realised the power of sleep. With no computers, minimal mobile devices and no television the whole family was in bed asleep by 9.30pm most nights.

Not much else changed. She was still exercising while away and eating as she had been, and drinking plenty of water but when she returned from the holiday having slept two hours a night more than normal, she had lost weight!

Needless to say she was astounded by just how powerful sleep and the hormonal rhythms of the body are.

Back To Brilliant
Step 3: Realign

The 'no pain, no gain' mentality of years gone by seems to be good for the short term but, potentially disastrous for long-term health and wellness.

Have you ever seen someone in the gym and instinctively thought: "That can't be good for you, can it?" as you see someone with poor posture and improper technique potentially making their posture worse as they strive to keep fit?

There are many occasions that I've seen a novice attempting an exercise that is too complex for their current level of fitness or postural stability. What happens when you continue to exercise like this? Over time you can create micro-traumas in the tissue or joints, which leads to injury. It's better to take a step back and slowly progress at a level that works for your body rather than 'feel the burn' and carry on regardless.

Total Gym, a US exercise equipment manufacturer surveyed a large number of personal trainers to find that 100% of them were working with at least one injured client. Injuries are common so using a traditional approach to keeping fit and healthy may require a different approach to improve these statistics.

Paul Chek, Founder of the *Chek Institute*, has developed a system of assessment and exercise prescription that is world class. This system offers a truly bespoke exercise programme that incorporates all your current injuries and weaknesses as well as a mean to strengthen and repair your body so you to pursue your goals.

Before you begin to rebuild a strong healthy physique, particularly if you're struggling currently with aches and pains, it is wise to adhere to the Chek Institutes hierarchy of what type of exercise should be performed and in what order.

In this *Realign* chapter I'd like to show you an evolutionary perspective on flexibility, stability and postural training. This will then provide a fantastic platform for building strength and an impressive physique outlined in the following section, *Rebuild*.

In Matthew Wallden's brilliant chapter, in the book, *Naturopathic Physical Medicine*, he puts forward the idea that various movements and systems of the human body have developed in response to the selective pressures of nature throughout the evolution of humankind, from single celled organisms millions of years ago to the complex interaction of systems of the human being.

This understanding of evolutionary development is useful when beginning to look at postural alignment, flexibility and stability. Without this understanding you might struggle to make lasting or meaningful change to your posture. And this understanding helps you lay down foundations for future training based on sound principles that complement your physiology and biology, not contradict it.

I have found that you can't safely and effectively build the levels of movement unless the preceding level is working soundly.

For example, a Level One movement is the most fundamental so Level Four movements cannot be utilised to their optimum without some form of trauma occurring to the tissues involved. As you saw from the graphs at the end of the last chapter, cumulative trauma should be avoided.

The structure below uses slightly different terminology to Matthew Wallden as I've found it easier to communicate to clients this way.

Level One
What Is It?

We must ensure that Level One is working correctly as it's the foundation of all movement. These muscles should be working pretty much constantly in your body to some degree. However if you're suffering with long-term aches and pains there is a good chance these muscles could be undermining optimal function.

Level One is made up of the deep abdominal muscles that live underneath the 'six pack' muscles you are no doubt familiar with and the digestive system. The digestive system and the deep abdominal muscles are made out of the same tissue when you were developing as a foetus! The same groups of nerves stimulate both systems.

In your mother's womb the tissue called the lateral plate mesoderm splits to become the deep abdominal muscles and the digestive system. *This is why what you eat is of paramount importance to the function of your abdominal muscles and why food also affects your spinal health.*

Stand or sit nice and tall and relax. Pull your belly button towards your spine.

The movement of pulling the belly button in towards the spine is what a Level One movement looks like at its most basic.

There are various types of this movement throughout the body such as swallowing or the actions of the digestive organs as it moves foods along through your system.

The muscle that you used to pull in the belly button is a hoop like muscle that surrounds the middle of your body, all the way around to the back.

Before any movement your belly button draws towards the spine. So if you bend over and pick up something from the floor your belly will very slightly pull towards the spine to stabilise you.

The slight movement of your pupil as it reacts to light, the contraction of your blood vessels and digestive tract are all examples of the Level One movements.

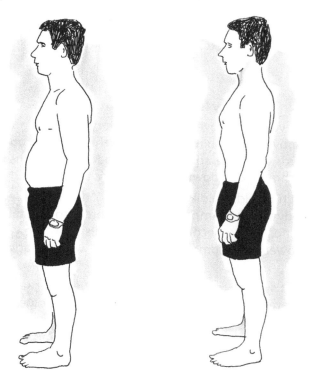

Evolution of Level 1

Level One movements are the most primal type of movement of all four levels. They are the first movements your body learns. The most ancient life forms on Planet Earth such as sea squirts or single cell amoeba are only able to move in this Level One pattern and it's from here that subsequent levels will build movement.

The muscle wall around the outside of the amoeba contracts and relaxes just like a hoop getting smaller and larger again. That's the only direction a hoop can move, toward or away from the centre.

From around five months after your conception, while still in the womb you began sucking your thumb and swallowing the amniotic fluid. This begins to stimulate the muscles in your body that contract in this Level One style and is pretty much all you got to practice until you were born into a field of gravity, which begins the next phase of development.

Why Is This Important to You?

The Level One movement is the very beginning of every single movement you make. It draws the belly button muscle in towards the spine, squashing the abdominal organs up into the diaphragm and down into the pelvic floor.

This action adds rigidity to the whole of the middle section of your body and most importantly contributes to the stability for your spine. It also decompresses or pulls apart the vertebrae in the lower back, something that helps with managing wear and tear.

If this system doesn't work very well because these muscles are weak, or you eat foods that upset your digestion, you increase the risk of back pain and actually many other types of body pain. For example, if you go running and this system works well the force of your foot landing on the ground will travel up the leg into the hip and up through the spine and the energy dissipates out the top of the head.

However if there is a weakness, the energy can become blocked because of incorrect sequencing of muscles and joint stability. The energy then is not dissipated effectively and can end up trapped at the knee, hip or the lower back, for example, running 5-10 kms after work to de-stress, can actually end up stressing your spine and causing greater problems.

If there is a weakness here, the energy could become blocked because of incorrect sequencing of muscles and joint stability. The energy then is not dissipated as it should be, most effectively.

How Does It Go Wrong?

The Level One movements can become dysfunctional in a number of ways such as physically with pain in the surrounding joints or muscles, constipation and poor breathing.

Food choices that cause bloating, gas or disruption to optimal digestion can also interfere with these basic internal movements.

And they can be disrupted mentally and emotionally. Emotional stress that causes an upset stomach is one example. If this happens fairly frequently, the muscles will become weaker.

The digestive system, as I said, is made of the same tissue as the deep abdominal muscles and therefore requires the digestive system to be working well. Bloating or other forms of disharmony in the digestive system can result in a distress signal to the nervous system filtering back to the muscles and hindering their function.

How You Make Sure It Works

Part of any corrective exercise programme to get your body working well should contain exercises that strengthen weak muscles and stretch tight muscles in a systematic way resulting in bio-mechanical harmony.

The key exercises for this area of the body are:

Four Point Tummy Vacuum

In the above position try taking a deep breath and let the abdomen out. As you breathe out and draw the belly button up towards the spine. Hold for ten seconds and repeat eight times. Take a 50 second break and built up to three sets.

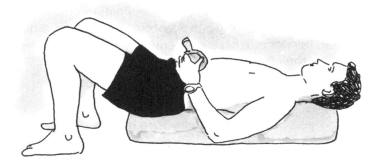

Diaphragmatic Breathing

Lay on your back and place a heavy book or bottle of water on your abdomen. Use this weight as feedback as you breathe in. Take deep breaths allowing the weight on top of your abdomen to rise and fall each time you breathe. The first two thirds of the breath should be in the abdomen and only the final third should move up into the chest.

Level 2
What Is It?

Level Two movements involve side to side motion. If you're standing upright and you slide your hand down your leg to touch the outside of your knee you are moving in this Level Two motion. This is the second movement you learn as a child, which you must master before you can graduate to more complex movements. As an adult your brain needs these first two systems to be working well before you start doing squats in the gym, running or playing golf, for example.

Evolution of Level 2

Level Two movements are seen through evolution when we progressed from sea squirts and single celled life forms to fish and reptile life. Think of a fish as it swims through water, side bending to create propulsion to move forwards or a lizard as it bends from one side to the other as it moves across the ground.

As I said, in the womb we learn how to carry out Level One movements by swallowing fluid and sucking our thumb, which ignites the use of the digestive system and deep abdominal muscles.

When we are born however, we now have a new challenge: gravity. The infant has to learn how to move with gravity pushing down on his/her little body 24 hours per day. This new form of stress requires developing a different type of movement to overcome the challenge.

The Level One type of movement was useful before but will not help the baby move around.

Babies move around and wriggle but in the first few months, they are not yet strong enough to resist gravity.

A lizard-like side to side movement is the most efficient style of movement at this stage of development and is part of the baby's strategy to wriggle around in a cot.

Why It's Important to You?

With the everyday movements you make in the Level Two side to side pattern, you benefit greatly by being stabilised so other muscles can also provide propulsion. For example, as you climb the stairs Level Two muscles inside and around the hip will stop the knees collapsing inward and damaging ligaments and cartilage.

How Does It Go Wrong?

When the Level One muscles become dysfunctional, as discussed, subsequent levels over compensate.

This can result in faulty movement patterns such as over using the arms or legs because the forces are not passing through the spine as they should, in what is know as a 'sling'. One example of a sling is how your left buttock muscles work with the muscles of the right side of your upper back into the right arm. This force crosses the spine, and also requires effective activation of the Level One muscles.

As well as faulty Level One movements, Level Two movements can also become faulty through poor exercise choices.

Machine-based exercise is said to be a common factor in the underdevelopment or de-conditioning of the Level Two muscles. Machine-based exercises and more generally, exercises that focus solely in front to back movements such as the bench press, result in little use of the Level Two muscles either to generate movement or to act as a stabiliser while the other muscles work.

How You Make Sure It Works

Strength and stability in these muscles can be obtained and maintained in a variety of ways, from single arm or leg exercises that load the spine in this one-sided way.

This is most exemplified is the exercise below:

Swiss Ball Side Flexion

Level 3
What Is It?

Level Three is all about movements from back to front. Bending straight forwards at the hip for example, is a Level Three movement. Mastering the forces of gravity on your spine in an upright position would first of all require you to be able to move in a front to back motion but on all fours (hands and knees). If you think you have poor posture it's possibly because you slouch too much. Slouching forward is a weakness or inability to hold yourself upright in this Level Three way.

Evolution of Level 3

In evolutionary terms the Level Three movement is seen best in mammals. They have mastered both levels One and Two and move themselves around in a more efficient way.

As an infant, once you mastered moving around like a lizard on your stomach the next, much faster way to get around was crawling on your hands and knees, like an animal on all-fours.

Crawling around on your hand and knees is where forces began to be applied through the shoulder joint and hip joints to harden the tissues in preparation for the next stage.

Why It's Important to You?

As an infant, crawling was a much faster, more efficient method of moving around than being on your stomach or back, yet until this point of development at around 12 months, you wouldn't have had the strength in the arms and legs to crawl.

This four-point position is a useful for rehabilitating an injured shoulder joint.

Exercises done in a four point position on the hands and knees allow the hip and shoulder joints to be loaded in such a way the main stress is placed through areas of thick bone development on the shoulder blade and pelvic bone.

This could be a throw back to having evolved from mammals on all fours, where over many thousands of years the bones developed to cope with such stress. We still have the remains of this bony development today.

If you're not able to stabilise your spine in good posture in the correct way, four point exercises will be a useful tool.

How Does It Go Wrong?

Firstly poor function of the basic levels will undermine adequate functional movements and lead to muscles becoming imbalanced with some muscles becoming over-developed and other becoming weaker.

For example poor Level One muscles can result in over-use of the six pack muscles. This over activity in the six pack muscle pulls the chest down and distorts the posture in the upper back. Imagine a hunched-over posture.

This position is also dysfunctional for your shoulders and can lead to shoulder and neck pain in the upper body

How You Make Sure It Works

All levels of movement offer a range of difficulty to match your needs in exercising each level. See the pictures below for three exercises dominant in the Level Three motion that progressively get more demanding.

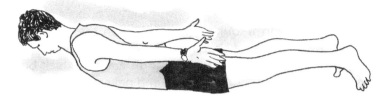

Prone Cobra

Weighted Hip Extension

Front Squat

Level 4
What Is It?

This is the ultimate expression of human movement, which is only possible if you have mastered all the previous levels and maintained your strength in all of them. This Level Four movement requires twisting type patterns. For example, if you tried to look behind you, your neck and back would have to twist to allow this movement.

Evolution of Level 4

When the selective pressures of natural development got to the point of evolution where mammals walked on their two hind legs, it became necessary to be able to twist to make full use of this upright position.

While there are small amounts of rotation in mammal's spines it's not until we get to humans in the evolutionary spectrum that we see significant rotation in the neck and upper and lower back regions.

In fact it's the rotation that ultimately means we can walk on two legs. With rotation and the increased capacity of the human nervous system to keep all levels of movement functional, we master bipedal gait with the ability to walk, jog and sprint.

Walking, jogging and sprinting requires significant development and maintenance, using the right exercises and lifestyle management to ensure these skills remain functional.

Why It's Important to You?

We also see that throwing comes in at Level Four as to throw an object effectively you must twist throughout your body.

Not twisting using the whole body will mean you 'over throw' from other parts of the body causing stress on these structures and possible injury in the longer term.

Therefore to rehabilitate a chronically painful shoulder can require that the twisting movement in the lower back is restored to make sure you don't suffer a recurring problem in the future. For that matter if your Level One, Two or Three muscles are not working you could well have a recurring problem and fail to get to the bottom of it.

I hope now you realise how to get yourself working effectively you have to really be functioning well at all levels of your body. Focusing on one part of the body over the others because that's where the symptoms show up is not the route to optimal health and fitness.

How Does It Go Wrong?

Asymmetrical movements such as kicking a football with the same leg repeatedly, swimming and only breathing to one side or a job with a poor position that must be maintained for hours can contribute to faulty functioning at Level Four.

This level requires significant control from your nervous system so head injuries, whiplash or learning difficulties can also contribute to this level having less functional bio-mechanics.

How You Make Sure It Works

Possibly the ultimate expression of Level Four movement is sprinting. This ability distinguishes humans from our aquatic, reptilian and mammalian ancestors. Walking, jogging and sprinting maintain condition in these muscles.

However they are not the only forms of exercise that can be used for the large muscles.

See the two clever exercises below that require all four levels to work harmoniously together.

Cable Push

Cable Pull

Posture - Aesthetics and Pain

A well-designed corrective exercise programme should balance your body and move you towards a position of ideal posture. This can take the strain from areas around joints and aligns your bones in the position of least stress.

By improving your posture, you improve your aesthetics immeasurably. It's one thing to improve how you look by adding muscle tissue but if you hurt and actually look unbalanced or out of proportion due to poor posture, is there any point? Someone with poor posture usually stands out in a crowd, for the wrong reasons. Someone with good posture carries a completely different energy, looking more powerful and authoritative.

Some interesting work by Amy Cuddy shows just how important posture can be to your hormonal system.

She observed certain power poses in differing arenas from sport to business and found that those who demonstrated skill and proficiency in their field moved and held certain postures. For example, a footballer's celebration of arms held aloft after scoring a goal or Usain Bolt's victory gesture as he crosses the finish line to win. She called them 'power poses' and studied their effect on the hormonal system.

She found that just holding a power pose for two minutes, like standing tall with you hands on the hips, can significantly increase testosterone and reduce cortisol, a major stress hormone.

Therefore if you stand, sit and move with good posture not only will you take the stress off the body, you'll also improve vital hormones for good health, muscles growth and repair and trigger sex hormone production.

Do you need more reasons to improve your posture?

Symmetry is Athletic

Symmetry is ideal when it comes to good posture. In fact this is the reason for having so many mirrors in gyms. They're not there for vanity. Viewing yourself in a mirror while exercising will help you maintain good technique and postures and symmetry.

Asymmetrical body postures can cause pain or pain can cause asymmetry. For example, if you slip a intervertebral disc you may be hunched over for a time in spasm and unable to stand with good posture until you regain comfort or seek professional help.

If you look in the mirror and one shoulder is higher than the other, your head tilts off to one side very slightly, one leg turns out more than the other or you notice one hand sits further forward on the body than the other, you're seeing an asymmetrical picture.

These physical quirks are clues to which muscles need stretching or strengthening with corrective exercise. You could end up with a programme of stretches for the left side of your body and strengthening exercises for the right. Making you more symmetrical will improve the way your body feels and improve function and your appearance. Who knows it might even increase your levels of testosterone and reduce stress hormones!

Right Place Right Time

When a joint is in good postural alignment and moves well, with symmetry throughout its motion it will be in the right place at the right time throughout this motion. This is known as *Optimal Instantaneous Axis of Rotation.*

Muscles go into spasm because the small, stabilising muscles around each little joint, lets say one of the vertebrae in the back, feed the message to the nervous system that the joint is in the wrong place at the wrong time during movement.

The primary job in that area then becomes to try and stabilise the vertebrae. This can result in the wrong muscles being switched on in an emergency to add stability to the area. These muscles are likely to remain relatively tense until stability is gained in the spine.

Reduced Wear and Tear

With good posture and the joints being in the right place at the right time during movement, there is significantly less wear and tear on them. The supporting structures are able to do their job and the forces going through the body, are then able to move as they should.

If you have poor posture and run, for example, you're dramatically increasing the chances of ankle, knee or back pain, because the force of landing multiplies your normal body weight many times over.

If forces travel through the body without being impeded, that is, you have optimal postural alignment, you'll stand a far greater chance of avoiding injury while exercising. If you've got knock knees, a flat lower back or forward head posture you might just be asking for trouble by pounding the pavements after work!

Rest Postures

Slouching on the sofa and sitting hunched over your laptop are ruining your back. The spinal discs take a beating when you're slumped over like that. Rest postures are based on the idea that if you use your body at rest during your normal day to day activities, as you would have done as a caveman, without chairs, beds, desks and sofas, you are using your body to help maintain its flexibility naturally.

When you see people in India happily sitting in a full squat position, they're getting a fantastic stretch on the calves, hips and knee joints, very naturally in a sustainable way.

I highly recommend you use these positions as often as is practical; particularly if you have very rigid, inflexible parts of your body. Over time, your rigid body will adapt to the natural positions and you will regain surprising levels of flexibility.

Using these rest postures with older clients in their 70's and 80's has enabled them to regain mobility they thought was just not possible. Not only does this alleviate pain and discomfort it can radically improve quality of life. If you are inflexible to the degree that you are uncomfortable, or that you're restricted in daily movements you'll find great benefit in these natural postures, I'm sure.

With each position, your body will let you know when it's time to move into another posture. It might feel uncomfortable to sit in a squat position for a minute but eventually will become easier.

It's worth remembering, you are made to move.

Movement pumps joints and the fluids around the joints so moving between a few different rest postures when your body tells you to do so is fine.

Try the ones that are easiest to build into your life and most practical for you. Once you get the benefits of one or two I'm sure you'll use more.

Long Sit

If you use the long sit to watch TV or read this will really improve and maintain good function around the hip and behind the knee.

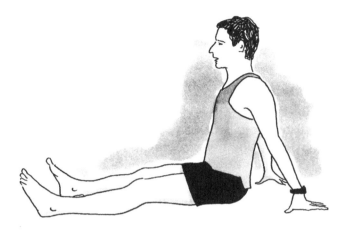

Front Laying

This is great if you want to read on the floor. If you feel the need to extend your back if you've been sitting in a chair all day, for example, this can be a reasonably gentle position to get into and rest in for a few minutes.

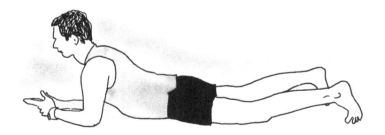

Cross Legged

Sitting cross legged may be difficult but if you persist the position will nicely open up your hips and allow a much greater range of motion, which will allow you to achieve many more positions for effective exercise. Stiff immobile hips often contribute to lower back pain.

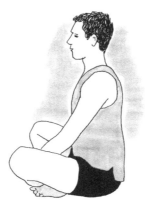

Low Kneeling

This is another position that is often quite tricky for some people and will take time to achieve if you're stiff across the ankles or knees. Persist and it will work wonders!

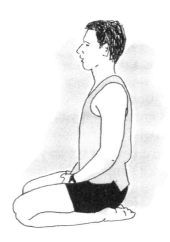

Full Squat

This is a fantastic position for the ankle, knee, hip and lower back to maintain or regain mobility. It's a highly functional position yet you may not even be able to get close to the full squat to start with. The other easier postures will help you to regain a level of flexibility and mobility needed to master this position.

When you begin to try the full squat position start slowly if you can't do it straight away. Pick something to sit on, like a stack of books, to allow you to get part way into the squat position with a slight effort but without discomfort.

See the three-staged progression below.

Working Posture

I'm sure you spend a reasonable amount of time at a desk on the computer during your working day. If not every day, some days at least. Understanding exactly how you should sit at the computer is important if you suffer with chronic neck, back and shoulder pain.

Even if you've had an expert set up your workstation or give advice before, I think it's important to review the picture on the next page.

Important points to take note of:

- The base of the chair should be level so it doesn't compress your weight into the back of the leg or the bottom. If it slopes slightly away from you or towards you there is a risk that pressure will cause sciatic pain. (that is, pain from the lower back down the leg)

- Your hip joint and back should form a 90 degree angle.

- Your arm should drop straight from your shoulder, you should not be reaching for the keyboard. And your elbows should be at a 90 degree angle.

- The centre of the screen should be at eye level. This is especially important when you are working on a laptop. It's best to buy a separate keyboard and raise the screen. Set up the separate keyboard appropriately on your desk.

- The lumbar support should be in the lumbar region. This seems obvious but I've seen lumbar supports been way out of place. The main support should be in line with the belly button if you imagine drawing a line straight through the body horizontally.

Reading Posture

If you suffer with chronic neck pain it's important to check the posture of your shoulders, neck and head. When doing reading work, particularly if it involves looking down toward a desk or table, you would really benefit by supporting the weight of your head in your hand. This will mean the hand is taking the weight of the head so the force is not traveling into the neck.

When possible bring reading materials up in line with your eyes rather than taking your head down towards the reading material. Doing it this way round can save wear and tear on your neck.

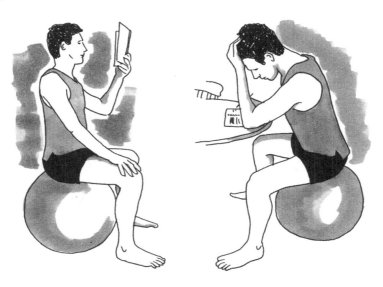

Back To Brilliant
Step 4: Rebuild

'Training intelligence' means using your body as it's meant to be used to get the absolute best from your body, naturally. If you stick to what the selective pressures of nature have designed you for, you'll develop a winning physique with relative ease and remain pain free.

Seven Movement Patterns

There are seven movements that your body does everyday without you even thinking about them, which are *lunge, squat, push, pull, bend, twist* and *gait* which has three variations: *walking, running* and *sprinting*.

Examples of you squatting during your normal daily activities would be getting down onto the toilet or getting into your car. As simple as it seems to get on the toilet, there are many people I have assessed over the years who were not able to perform this fundamental movement.

To then go into a gym and use a leg press machine to strengthen the legs or use a bar to perform squats with a trainer might make your back hurt or stiffen muscles that are already too tight. Sometimes these imbalances are one-sided, which can create even more stress.

For example, you may deviate off to one side as you sit down stressing the lower back and hip joint.

Ideally, before any exercise, a proficient assessment should be performed to discover which of these patterns of movement are deficient and which are at a functional standard.

My job is to find what's restricting the ideal movement and then restore that movement pattern and get you doing it really well, automatically. The squat example is only one; there are daily examples of all the movements I've identified.

In essence mastering these movements and using them to base your training around will mean you hit every muscle you have in your body, therefore achieving a brilliant body with nothing over or under developed.

Balanced exercise programmes are hugely important if you wish to stay healthy, avoid pain and look at your best, for the long term. Therefore it's vital to perform correctly an adequate mix of the movements below to achieve a great body.

Lunge   Squat

Bend

Twist

Push

Pull

Gait

Gait is made up of walking, running and sprinting.

The difference being the speed of these movements. There can be imbalances that show up when running that are not evident when sprinting or walking, because each one has its own motor programme in the brain.

The three modes of gait utilise different energy systems too, depending on the speed at which they are completed:

- Walking - aerobic (meaning energy produced by oxygen intake)
- Running - aerobic if slow enough, or anaerobic (meaning energy produced from stores within the muscles) Think the 400 - 800 meter events in athletics.
- Sprinting - neural/ATP (as with fast running, adenosine triphosphate is used within the muscle, but the downside with this energy system is its used up within 12-15 seconds.) Think the 100 meters event in athletics.

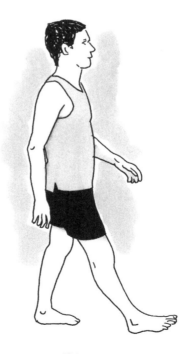

Running

Sprinting

The Training Blend

Your training blend ideally should always contain some form of muscle building work, endurance work for cardiovascular benefits, speed and power work and heavy maximal weight lifting. These are again functional components that will be present in your activities of daily living, whether you are fully aware or not. Therefore to remain pain free and get the absolute best from your body you need to practise the right blend of movements.

There are also other abilities that should be part of your varied exercises to keep your nervous system highly tuned.

Balance training can be incorporated into exercises to train your body with the ability to respond to unstable surfaces, for example. While you may come across a patch of ice very infrequently, it only takes one fall on ice or a wet floor, to cause a break or sprain to your hip or wrist that changes the function of your body for life and impacts your quality of living. Including this balance training can keep the nervous system in tune and therefore buy you precious milliseconds to respond accordingly, to right your centre of gravity and avoid such an injury.

Using Swiss balls and other balance type apparatus in gyms activates reflexes that are not stimulated when you are on more stable surfaces such as a bench or even a machine.

Muscle Builds Metabolism

The technical name for this is hypertrophy, which means increasing the size of your muscles. Aside from making you feel good when you look in the mirror there are other benefits to muscles such as greater resting metabolism. Here's a list of benefits to having increased toned muscle on your body:

- Increased metabolic rate
- Supports and protects joints
- Reduced risk of type 2 diabetes

- Greater joint stability
- Reduced risk or chronic joint pain
- Improved hormonal balance

You need a heart for endurance training

When you think of endurance you may be thinking of long distance running, cycling or swimming but these are cyclical methods of how to include endurance into your programme.

Your best bet when it comes to endurance is to use strength endurance in your training blend as this allows you to maintain more muscle tone throughout your body compared to the cyclical examples above.

It also helps you work on postural muscles if you target them well with a structured programme, so that you are supplementing any rehabilitation work you may have done and keeping the postural alignment of your body as close to optimal as possible.

Long distance running, swimming and cycling can all produce unfavourable postural imbalances leading to pain and instability, if done in isolation without postural training to supplement.

Using the movement patterns we've looked at already you are getting a wider mix of movement vocabulary in different planes of motion (side to side, back to front and twisting), unlike cycling for example which is very dominant in the back to front plane of motion with minimal twisting or side to side movement.

Speed & Power

Speed and power are very much over looked and you'll benefit hugely from adding this type of training into your training blend when the time is right for you. Getting the foundations laid with your Level One to Four basics first before progressing onto these moves will allow you to benefit from speed and power exercises without taking steps backwards due to injury.

This is where your training can start to look more sport specific and the benefits of the cross over are, if you do play occasional sports, you won't be laid up injured after a small game of weekend rugby, football or a round of golf.

The Big Lifts

The big lifts are those that you use when you have mastered all the basics of the Levels One to Four movements in the previous section and started doing some speed and power work.

This is brilliant work for increasing the anabolic (rebuilding) hormones in the body, especially when you're older than 40 as these hormones begin to drop off after this age.

Typically with the big lifts you keep the number of repetitions in each set very low. For example, one to four repetitions of a deadlift would be a good 'big lift' exercise.

Here are some interesting points on what this could do for you:

- Improved self confidence
- Increase human growth hormone
- Increase IGF-1 hormone (important repair type hormone)
- Increased testosterone
- Reduced cortisol (chief inflammatory hormone)
- Increased metabolic rate
- Improved brain function
- Improved coordination
- Reduced rate cardiovascular disease
- Increased bone density

Avoiding Overload

More specifically, pattern overload is where you repeat movements so frequently that you cause excess stress to an area of the body, which leads to injury.

This can happen easily when using machines to exercise as they keep you in a fixed position and force a range of motion into your joints that may not be ideal for your body. If you then keep doing the same programme on the same machines over and over the muscles and joint tissues will become aggravated and ultimately become painful.

How do you avoid pattern overload? That's quite easy really!

By mastering the relevant movement patterns I have presented here in this chapter you will be using natural movements that will be maintained by adequate function of the many different muscles that all work simultaneously. If certain muscles become fatigued if you're doing a push up, for example, you may move minimally, into a slightly different position on the way up to not use the fatigued muscle fibres.

On a machine, you can't do that because the axis of movement is fixed by the machine and the fatigued fibres would become overly stressed and possibly injure or stress the other structures around the joint.

Corrective Exercise

Corrective exercise, the way I teach, is the process of assessment, programme design and delivery of the best possible programme to firstly achieve your goals while simultaneously bringing the body back into balance.

It enables you to correct any faulty movements you may have developed so you can comfortably complete the base movements and limit the chance of trauma to tissue.

If you remember from the two graphs, poor posture and bio-mechanics can lead to increased rates of trauma at certain joints.

Corrective exercise analyses what the weakness and restrictions are and puts a plan of action in place.

Without thorough assessment it becomes increasingly difficult to write a programme that is ideal for you. Why? Well because the body contains complex systems that are all constantly interacting. When a thorough holistic assessment is completed it's possible to see more than just the biomechanics that are out of balance.

These things are simply giving clues as to what is happening "under the bonnet" if you like. That is, the mental, emotional and lifestyle traits that begin to show up externally.

If a brilliant physique is about being pain free and symmetrical, so you look great on the outside and importantly, feel good on the inside, then how can this be achieved without first knowing where you are starting from? Which muscles are short and tight and therefore need stretching? Which muscles are long and weak and therefore need strengthening?

Your ideal programme is one that ultimately leaves you stretching only the tight muscles and strengthening the weak ones.

Think about it like tuning up a guitar. Some strings (muscles) need to be tighter and some need to be slightly looser to make it play in tune. If you don't tune it properly all you get is noise not music. Would you say your body is making music or noise most of the time? What makes you say this?

Corrective exercise, applied well, can help you achieve your goals and make you look and feel brilliant again.

How an Assessment Works

You come to see us and we guide you through all of the movement and postural assessments and take notes on your work and home situations too. You might work at a desk most of the time and spend a few nights a week watching television to relax with the family.

Each morning before getting into the shower you do 25 push ups and 25 sit ups to 'keep on top of things' and occasionally you do some star jumps to get your heart rate up.

You do all of these movements for us and we notice:

- During the push up your right shoulder hikes up toward your ear as you go down towards the floor.
- Your knees buckle in towards one another as you jump up and down during the star jumps.
- Your upper abdominals are much stronger than the lower abdomen and there is an imbalance.

Although you said that you wanted to have a flat stomach as one of your primary goals when you came in, much to your surprise, we ask you to stop doing sit-ups each morning! What's more the push-ups are also knocked on the head.

Below is what your programme might look like:

Exercise/Stretch	Instructions
Swiss Ball Abdominal Stretch	Lay on your back on the ball for 90 seconds
Neck Stretch	Stretch the Right side only - 60 seconds hold
Chest Stretch	Face down arm on ball - 60 seconds each side
Swiss Ball Prone Row	3 x 15 repetitions - hold for 2 seconds at the top
Prone Cobra	3 x 60 seconds hold at the top

Stretching Before Not After

There are so many schools of thought on when to stretch, what to stretch, why bother stretching at all and so on. The view I take is founded upon a very clear physiological law called, the *law of facilitation.*

In plain English it basically says if a muscle is short and tight it will continue to be short and tight even if you exercise the opposing muscles to pull it in the other direction. Essentially the brain is sending an impulse along the path of least resistance.

There is an interesting case of a well respected physiotherapist who had many students return to him and say that they'd been doing the exercises he taught them with their back pain patients without seeing results.

They decided to assess what the relevant muscles were doing during each exercise by measuring the electrical impulses given off by the muscles.

Each time these patients were doing the back exercises the abdominal muscles were giving off the electrical signal, showing the path of least resistance for that person. Being surprised by this, they then stretched the abdominal muscles and did the exercise again with a very different result; the back muscles now received the signal.

This experiment showed it is best to stretch before you exercise and not afterwards. Stretch the short, tight muscles that can over ride what you're trying to achieve, then exercise the long weak muscles and you'll be in great shape.

Technique

You must have excellent technique in all your exercises. There is no excuse for doing an exercise with poor technique. If you are unable to perform an exercise with the required technique then it must be made one level easier so you can actually use the muscles you are meant to be using. If you can't do it well then you're not benefiting your body.

Your technique might falter after doing some of the exercise well in the preceding sets. The trick is learning when you start to fatigue and stopping, ideally before you can no longer keep your body in the correct positions. This is where a good coach comes into their own, spotting the sign of fatigue and working you up to that point but not beyond it.

There's Always a Way

All exercises can be scaled to your needs and abilities from the most basic of rehabilitation or Pilates type exercise to the most complex power-lifting movements.

The skill is in having your ability assessed and understanding exactly what level you need to be working at.

The examples I gave you in the Seven Movement Patterns section are a small sample of how each movement can be scaled. For example, for someone with a back injury, let's say a disc complaint, the squat movement can be scaled back all the way to laying on the floor on your back, slowly working toward a full body weight squat.

How Long and How Often

I have a rule that if you follow, will allow you to make amazing changes in your body without being in the gym for hours, freeing you to spend time doing other things. Many people are surprised when I say a small amount is all you really need to do. The cliché, 'less is more' certainly does apply to resistance training.

Spending 30 minutes hard work three times per week plus 10-15 minutes of stretching daily is all you need.

Keeping the corrective stretching session short is practical and allows you to make big strides in regaining your balance and achieving a brilliant physique.

30 minutes of hard work is all I do and I get great results. Your 30 minute workout might look like this circuit below:

Exercise	Instructions	Time
Squat	5 x 10 repetitions/ 40 seconds rest between each set	7 minutes 5 seconds
Pull Up	5 x 10 repetitions/ 40 seconds rest between each set	7 minutes 5 seconds
Lunge	5 x 10 repetitions/ 40 seconds rest between each set	7 minutes 5 seconds
Push Up	5 x 10 repetitions/ 40 seconds rest between each set	7 minutes 5 seconds

Total = 28mins 20sec

It's been shown that the fight/flight system is overly active after approximately 30 minutes of vigorous working out so there are little gain to be had doing more than that anyway. Keep it simple and keep it to 30 minutes or less.

If you are not feeling fully worked out after this time then you're either not working hard enough, underestimating how hard you could work, not doing the correct technique or have the wrong level of exercise for your needs.

Consistency Is King

Consistency is what you need to achieve an ideal body shape and transform yourself from constant niggles, aches and pains to a brilliant body. As I've said, you don't have to be obsessed with the gym and exercising or food. You do, however, need to be consistent and continuously making progress.

Your body will begin breaking muscle tissue down within 72 hours so sporadic exercise sessions here and there just won't do it. Two times per week is fine if that's all that you can manage but you'll make very slow progress and will only go so far on that. This is why I say three times per week is ideal.

Now at this point, I must also emphasise that I don't mean three times per week hard and fast every single week of the year. Just like any professional athlete your training should go through cycles of harder periods and easier periods; weeks where you tapper back and work on your weaknesses and other weeks where you utilise your potential and give it everything you've got.

'Super compensation' is the process of your body getting worse or weaker following a training session then your body rebuilds itself over the next 24-48 hours to be able to withstand the same amount of stress again next time.

So for 24 hours if you did the same programme you'd not perform quite as well as you did the first time. Then your body rebuilds, plus a little extra, and you're ready to perform again at an even better level. Consistency is important as you start to get weaker and lose muscle tissue if you leave it too long between exercise sessions. As I said, around the 72 hour mark is ideal between sessions.

Daily Stretch

If you suffer with chronic pain in your back, neck or shoulders, you will benefit hugely from stretching if you get into a routine of 10 -15 minutes daily; stretching the appropriate muscles of course.

Your body adapts to the stresses you put it under and the training, ergonomics and other activities of your daily life influence your body's function. It's very natural to stretch. Animals are quite often seen stretching and they constantly move, which is a form of mobility exercise in itself. Sitting at a desk, in meetings or behind a computer in a coffee shop sending emails will ultimately take its toll.

The following three stretches are very useful after periods at the computer and I highly recommend you do them if you work at a desk every day.

Long Lie

The long lie is the easiest stretch in the world. You need a six inch foam roller and you lay on it length ways with your arms out to the side, palms up.

This opens the chest, relaxes the back and allows you also to practice your diaphragmatic breathing, while also decompressing the intervertebral disks which under pressure while seated.. You need to stay in the position for a minimum of three minutes but anywhere up to 10 minutes would be good.

Hamstring Stretch

When you sit all day with your legs bent at the knee it can frequently lead to tension in the hamstring muscles that run down the back of your leg; particularly behind the knees.

Place a rolled towel under your lower back, at belly button level. Roll it to the thickness of your hand as this keeps the curvature of the lower back as it should be. Place your hands round the leg and pull the toes back toward you shin as much as possible. Now straighten the leg and hold it for 60-90 seconds, each leg.

Neck Extensors

Forward head posture is a real problem with neck, shoulder and back pain and can contribute to tight hamstrings so it's well worth doing this stretch.

Stand against the wall to keep good alignment throughout the rest of your body or make sure you sit tall. Place one hand on the back of your head and one on the chin. Keeping the back of your head against the wall use the hand on the chin to draw the chin down toward the neck. Warning: don't allow the head to move forwards, just rock it on the same axis. Again hold for 60-90 seconds.

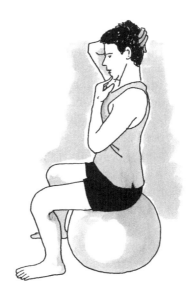

Getting Creative

Your workouts are only limited by your creative thinking. There is never an excuse to not exercise, at least to some extent. If you're on holiday and you don't have equipment you have your body! If you're traveling abroad with work you have the option of taking a case that is a good size to use as a weight and do what you can with the case. If the bed is moveable in your room you can always try picking it up a few times to practice your bending type movement patterns!

In all seriousness, the more creative you can get the better your workouts will be. You'll hit different muscles that your regular workouts just don't access and stimulate your enthusiasm if that has started to wane slightly.

What do you have around the house that allows you to exercise? In the garage? In the cellar or loft? There will be objects that are perfect for using to help you exercise. Even a chair can be made into a useful piece of kit.

Do What You Love

At the end of the day, you now know how to listen to the messages of your body. You have some basic tips to respond to what your body is telling you and motivation to keep going. But, if you don't like the form of exercise you do regularly and you only do it because you think you should, your resolve won't last. It will be great while you're motivation is high but on the down days you'll skip bits, if you bother at all.

What could you do that you love doing that is also exercise? What type of exercise do you love doing? When do you love doing it and with who? If you can do enjoyable activities more often with a friend or training buddy then you'll have fun and stick to it long term.

Whatever you choose, commit for the long term. Make it a habit and keep going. Your body will be much better off for it in the long run and getting the body shape you want will be easier and more sustainable.

Back To Brilliant
Step 5: Recover

Have you ever spent more money in a month than you earned? I'm guessing like most people you have. Have you ever done that for a number of months in a row and lived with a credit card debt that needed paying back? Again like most people I'm sure you have your own version of that story.

The point is, you paid the money back, irrespective of when you paid it back, you did or you had a plan to do so.

In many ways your body is like the bank you owed money to. You can borrow from the *Body Bank* but it must be repaid if you are to maintain adequate health and wellbeing.

Homeostasis, the point of equilibrium for all body systems, is the holy grail your body constantly seeks. However this is a theoretical point as the human body is constantly in flux. If you get too warm your body will begin to sweat in an attempt to cool you down. If you become hungry your body will signal to you to eat to maintain adequate levels of blood sugar. These are automatic systems aimed at maintaining the equilibrium.

The energy of your body is much the same. There are times during your day, week or month when you have more energy and times when you have less, no doubt. An incredibly common observation with clients aiming to achieve optimal health and wellbeing is a desire to exercise when the body is out of balance energetically. In my opinion exercise is a tool that can be used to optimise your body, if used wisely.

Used with more awareness, exercise can effectively help you maintain or obtain your equilibrium point and therefore optimal health and fitness. Used incorrectly there is a progressive worsening of the imbalanced state of wellbeing.

For example, just like a credit card debt where you pay off the balance, you must also pay off the energetic balance when you are not at your optimal best.

You can spend more money when you have the money in your bank account to spend. You can also exercise hard and increase fitness levels when you have energy in reserve to spend.

Why would you think it possible to get optimal results with you health and fitness programme if you exercise hard, despite having a poor night's sleep, getting up early to catch the 'red eye' flight, eating on the run during a busy day in and out of meetings, on top of your high blood pressure?

In our financial analogy, does this sound like having a positive balance? Or does it sound like a debt that needs repaying?

So what are you supposed to do if you are experiencing levels of stress and you have a busy life, with the elements I've described that need accounting for?

You might say that a day like that warrants a day of rest from the gym? But what if that ends up being a trend and all you ever really feel ready for is a day of rest? Where does that end? That certainly will not help with your plan to get fit and healthy. After all the *World Health Organisation* recommends a minimum of 20 minutes of physical activity each day.

I personally believe that life really is about movement, without movement you would find it very difficult to maintain your equilibrium point for all the systems of the body.

Your bones for example, would not get as much compressive force as needed and therefore weaken over time. Compression is a benefit of weight training. And there are energetic benefits of movement that may go unseen.

Piezo electricity is the energy that is produced by your body by simply moving. You might want to think of this as free energy, like an electric dynamo. You move and the body charges itself up with energy to be used at a later date. However if you move too vigorously you'll use the Piezo electric charge and some of the stored energy.

Again much like our credit card analogy you are going to go into energetic debt if you are already low on reserves and moving around too vigorously, which is a good indicator to slow down, not push harder!

So, what can you do for 20-40 minutes a day that would help you restore your equilibrium while still moving your body, if vigorous movement would only deplete you further?

The *Recover* step of the 5R process aims to show you how to be observant of your *Body Bank* and how to make an assessment of what you need on any given day to move your body back towards a balanced, optimal point.

In Part Three you'll also find some actionable steps for when your *Body Bank* is in debt and needs recharging.

Optimal Health

$$\longleftarrow \qquad\qquad\qquad \longrightarrow$$

Low reserves	*Over active*
Feeling burnt out	*Long days*
Picking up colds easily	*Hyper state*
Depressed state	*Body overheats*
Cold body temperature	*Increased adrenal function*
Reduced adrenal function	*High blood pressure*
Dizzy when getting up	

You have three hormones that keep you alive. These primary hormones are:

Cortisol

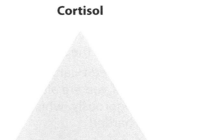

Adrenaline   **Insulin**

Cortisol

Cortisol is your chief anti-inflammatory agent, so when inflammation occurs its job is to reduce the levels of inflammatory agents and help restore a balance.

Anti-inflammatory drugs are the number one most consumed drug worldwide today.

A few examples of why inflammation might occur are:

- Stress at work or home
- Consumption of foods you're are intolerant to
- Consuming alcohol on an empty stomach

Adrenaline

Adrenaline is responsible for regulating the blood flow to muscle, making you feel alert and ready to get up and go. When someone is suffering with low adrenal function they can feel very sluggish and everything is an effort. If you wake up feeling drained and unrested, you might have low adrenaline levels.

Insulin

Insulin is your blood sugar hormone. It helps you maintain a healthy level of glucose in the blood at all times and assists the other two hormones.

Like adrenaline insulin can play a key role in the fight-flight stress response. If your body thinks there's an emergency you'll need fuel to cope with it. Insulin helps to release stored glucose from muscles and the liver and release it back into the blood.

Consuming meals that are inadequate for your needs in respect of protein, carbohydrate and fat will ultimately affect your insulin levels. Eating according to your metabolic type as discussed in the *Rebalance* section and eating every four hours is a healthy habit for your insulin levels.

Now you know a little about the primary hormones and why they are important to you, I'll show you how to use these hormones to indicate whether your *Body Bank* is full or running on empty.

The *Body Bank Calculator* is designed for pre-exercise so you can make an assessment of what you should be doing on any given day and how hard you might want to push yourself. It uses the primary hormones as the marker for how close or far away from equilibrium you are at the time.

The Body Bank Calculator

Pick the answer that best applies to you and be as brutally honest as you can.

Total your scores and check the table for your *Body Bank* calculation:

I ate my last meal:

- 90 minutes to two hours ago (0 points)
- Three to four hours ago (3 points)
- Less than 60 minutes ago (5 points)
- More than four hours ago (5 points)

Today my body feels like:

- No aches and pain from a previous exercise session and no low laying body pains (0 points)
- Mild aches from a previous exercise session (3 points)
- Discomfort in one area of the body that is less than a 5/10 on a pain scale (5 points)
- Discomfort in one or more areas of the body that is greater than a 5/10 on a pain scale (10 points)

Last night I slept for:

- 8-9 hours (0 points)
- 7-8 hours (3 points)
- 6-7 hours (10 points)
- Less 6 hours (20 points)
- More than 9 hours (5 points)

My energy on a scale of 1-10 is:

- 8-10 (0 points)
- 6-7 (5 points)
- Less than 6 (20 points)

Today I feel:

- Positive/Happy/Peaceful/Reassured/Grounded/ Confident/ (0 points)
- Ecstatic/Overflowing with positivity/Buzzing (3 points)
- Very slightly off centre/pensive/ (3 points)
- Mild anxiety/jealousy/anger/guilt/grief/sadness/ depression (5 points)
- Emotionally drained/Low/Anxious/Full of grief, anger, guilt, jealousy or sadness (10 points)

My level of stress at home today feels:

- Very low/virtually nothing (0 points)
- Manageable (3 points)
- Moderately stressing (5 points)
- Reasonably high (10 points)

My level of stress at work today feels:

- Very low/virtually nothing (0 points)
- Manageable (3 points)
- Moderately stressing (5 points)
- Reasonably high/Under pressure (10 points)

Your Body Bank Balance

- **Score of 0 - 15**
  Your body is well balanced today and you have sufficient reserves to exercise up to high levels intensity should you wish to.

- **Score of 16 - 35**
  Your body is showing moderate signs of debt that is building up either today if you're having an 'off' day or this could be an indicator of a longer term imbalance. *Go to the Body Bank Modification section at the end of Part 3 to see how to modify your exercise today.*

- **Score of 36 - 85**
  Your body is showing significant signs of debt being built up either today if you're having a very stressful day or this could be an indicator of a longer term imbalance. *Go to the Body Bank Modification section at the end of Part 3 to see how to modify your exercise today.*

Habits for a Good Body Bank Balance

There are certain lifestyle habits that help to maintain a good balance in the *Body Bank* and help you recover from the rigours of daily life. Below are three such examples:

Epsom Salts

Epsom salts are high in the compounds magnesium and sulfate both of which play an important role in your body's function.

If you're not eating right for your body's nutritional needs there's a good chance that you'll be deficient in magnesium, which is the third most abundant mineral in your body, giving you some indication of its importance.

Here is some important information about magnesium:

- All hormones are affected by optimal levels of magnesium (including growth hormones and testosterone)
- Detoxification pathways rely on optimal levels of magnesium particularly for balancing testosterone and estrogen.
- Low magnesium results in the mismanagement of insulin levels. This ultimately compromises adequate blood sugar regulation.
- You can become hyper reactive to stress with a magnesium deficiency.

Using Epsom salts in a bath a few times per week is a fantastic way of relaxing whilst topping up your magnesium levels and experiencing all the benefits above.

Earthing

Earthing is another very simple way to help your body recover naturally, sustainably and effortlessly.

Electrical items need earthing and so do humans. As with Piezo electricity, you are a bio-electrical battery charging and discharging all the time. The earth carries a negative electrical charge, which can be very useful. When you make contact with the earth you increase the negative charge in your body.

However the earth is clever, because if you already have an excessive negative charge the earth will absorb that excess from you. Importantly excessive electrons, which produce a negative charge can cause inflammation. If you are positively charged to the extent that you are out of optimal balance for your natural bio-electrical state the earth will balance you with its reserves of negative charge.

The soles of the feet have large amount of nerve endings so standing on grass in your garden is a great way to increase the negative charge should you need it.

Why is it a good idea to get your bare feet on the ground in your back garden?

The oxidation of cells greatly increases the rate at which it ages and promotes a dis-ease state. Science has newly found evidence on the importance of our bodies need for antioxidants.

Free radicals play a role in increasing the oxidation rate of cells. Free radicals are particles missing an electron and are the by products of mental/emotional stress, city living, over exposure to electrical devices and poor diets containing foods full of toxins. Environmental toxins and day to day living also produce free radicals, therefore in a way you could say they themselves are natural.

Free radicals become a problem when the antioxidants within your body are insufficient to neutralise a build-up.

Antioxidants provide this electron that free radicals are missing and help to reduce oxidation, reduce the ageing process of cells and create a healthy internal environment; reducing dis-ease states and protecting against the five things that kill us most frequently in the UK; cancer, heart disease, diabetes, strokes and accidents.

Getting your feet on the ground and absorbing some electrons to cancel out the free radicals running around your body after a stressful day, is one of the easiest ways to improve your life. Can you make that a habit?

Brain State

You have four main brain wave states, *Beta, Alpha, Theta* and *Delta*. Below are attributes of each:

- **Beta** - Awake and normal levels of alertness.
  Also associated with an overactive mind, stress, anxiety and frustration.

- **Alpha** - A peaceful state associated with rest and relaxation. You might be in this state if you are day dreaming or doing a light meditation.

- **Theta** - At this level you may drift into light sleep. But, this level is also connected with deep meditative states, creative insight and memory enhancement.

- **Delta** - Deep levels of sleep associated with non-REM and essential for full restoration of the immune system and maintenance of health in general.

The more time you spend in the Beta brainwave state the less likely you are to get adequate levels of Delta deep restorative sleep.

In the Sleep section on *Rebalance*, if you answered that you need 10-12 hours of sleep to feel fully rested then it's possible you are processing too much at the Beta brainwave level.

The more time you spend in the Beta state the more likely you are to burn yourself out. It's not a bad place to be, clearly, as this mental state allows you to be focused and get things done. However you might be spending too much time in Beta and not getting into a Delta brainwave state for enough time in your typical 24 hour day.

I can get stuck in Beta and find myself 'addicted' to thinking. I've discovered that Qigong is amazingly powerful for balancing such a state and creating a more favourable state for deep restorative sleep.

Rushing from place to place with lots of commitments, meetings and tasks to get done can create a dependence on the clock and as Ken Cohen says in, *The End of Stress*, a *'hurry syndrome'.*

In the Beta state, we are inducing a fight/flight response yet there really is nothing to flee or fight!

Hurry Syndrome is stress and stress pushes you out of balance.

Adaptogens are herbs that balance your physiology. Qigong can be regarded as an adaptogenic exercise, that is, whether the brainwave state is too slow or too quick it will promote an optimal state for balanced healthy function.

Quick Exercise

Here is my take on one of Ken Cohen's short relaxation exercises.

Sit upright away from the back of your chair, close your eyes and rest you hands in your lap.

First of all become aware of your breathing. Allow the breath to move in and out without any effort at all.

Allow the breath to breathe you.

Now imagine you're sat in the middle of a white fluffy cloud, pure white. Each breath in you breathe through the nostrils some of this white mist. Follow it all the way down to the base of the spine. Allow it to rise up through the spinal column and enter your head.

See it swirling around the head and cleansing the dark space there.

When you're ready breathe out darkened mist, possibly black. Repeat this for five minutes only with each breath cleansing the mind progressively.

After only five minute you'll notice a sense of relaxation and calm that perhaps was not there before. You'll have moved the brainwave state towards the Alpha state mentioned above.

Additional benefits of doing such an exercise include:

- Reduced muscle tension, chronic pain and blood pressure
- Increased energy
- Improved memory
- Strengthens the immune system
- Improved concentration levels

Part 3

Making *Brilliant* Happen

Making Brilliant Happen

There are some potentially life-changing ideas in this book. But ideas without action will not produce your desired outcome. Unless you act on these ideas they will remain just that, ideas. You're already very busy I would guess, as I am.

With feedback from clients and personal trial and error over the last 10 years or so, I have found that taking on projects and trying to change anything, be that body weight, your bank balance, getting rid of back pain or improving your level of happiness can be like spinning plates.

Plate spinning is incredibly skillful but some people can do it with relative ease. Do you know someone who seems to manage lots of things in their life yet rarely looks flustered? They achieve their goals, they appear happy and calm on the outside and carry an air of positivity and groundedness about them that seems infectious!

Well, I liken this to having their plates spinning and being in 'maintenance mode', that is, the plates have enough momentum to not fall and all they require is a little attention every now and again to maintain the momentum that stops them from crashing to the ground.

The opposite looks like this; you pick up one plate struggle to get it spinning and then decide to look for another plate, as you think it must be easier with a different type of plate but you also keep trying to spin the original plate too, you won't allow it to beat you. You break a few and are left standing flustered and with a few plates spinning but out of control and needing lots of attention. Been there? Done that?

I'll admit it, I've been there and it's no fun. The lack of balance the plates depict in this metaphor is possibly reflecting a lack of balance in an area of your life, perhaps many areas?

No matter how many plates you may have allowed to fall before, you can make peace with that. We have all dropped our plates and it will happen again I'm sure. We all make mistakes. However, the rest of the book will hopefully help you to set some priorities and choose one plate and get that spinning well and into 'maintenance mode' before you choose to pick up the next and learn to get that one into maintenance mode.

What is Maintenance Mode?

Maintenance mode is like brushing your teeth. Think back to when you were young and mum or dad were teaching you how to brush your teeth by yourself. The toothpaste goes all over the place, up the side of your mouth, some dribbles down your chin and it's generally quite a messy business!

However over time this task becomes simple you think about other things while brushing your teeth because it's automatic. Its well drilled into your behaviour. This is *maintenance mode*, the automatic.

It requires less conscious effort at this stage and you become subconsciously competent at the task, it just happens.

Establishing a level of conscious competence, that is, you're thinking about it, requires more energy.

Of the ideas that you've enjoyed in this book which do you think will be the most relevant for you to start with? Try listing everything that was useful to you while reading this book:

1.

2.

3.

4.

5.

Using your gut instinct, what feels like it would help you the most on the list you've made? Prioritise your list.

Whatever you consider your Number One priority, this is the most important 'plate' for you at the moment. When that one is up and spinning and in maintenance mode then it might be time to move onto the second new habit on the list.

Who likes to complete tasks, 'get stuff done'?

If you are, you might find that this more 'tortoise' approach is alien to you. I would simply ask you to consider how you normally feel with your existing strategy for 'getting stuff done'? You may well be an achiever but at what expense? Do you feel you need a month off when you've finished a project or completed an event because you're so burnt out?

If you get your emotional needs met by being the achiever type, you may also want to consider the SUCCESS Goal Setting formula, mentioned in Part 2.

This can help uncover what the achievement of the tasks/ change means to a part of your psyche.

Driving yourself into the ground is not a sustainable way to live and what's more it's not fun! Surviving on coffee or sugar, alcohol or needing pain killers might just be a warning sign for health issues more serious in the long run.

Ask for Help

Helping relationships are powerful when you're trying to change your behaviours and patterns. For getting things done and following through, if there is someone to help you hold yourself accountable, it can transform your goal setting and achievement experience.

Why do I say *someone to help you hold yourself accountable*?

If you ask a friend, colleague or partner to help you with a weekly check-in with your progress, a bit of motivation on a down day or a pat on the back on a good day it might also become dis-empowering and have the opposite effect in the long term.

Why? If the person helping is good at punishing you when you don't get something done or turn up late for an agreed training session, for example, they take on the position of parenting you.

If they become the Annoyed Parent it polarised you into the Naughty Child position and this is disempowering for your Adult psyche.

Questions are a hugely powerful tool and if you are considering asking someone for help, as a training buddy, an accountability partner or coach, is it someone who knows how to ask well directed questions to allow you to work the answers out for yourself? Do they help the authentic you blossom or do they want to bolster their own ego through control, punishment or more surprisingly by sabotaging your efforts?!

A good coach is worth their weight in gold and can help you uncover the brilliant elements of you screaming to get out from inside!

Essentialism

The 80/20 rule is one of my favourite principles in respect of getting things done and making changes. How can you do less and get more done? Be more productive and not get overwhelmed?

In the words of Greg McKeown, author of *Essentialism*, "It's about challenging the core assumption of 'we can have it all' and 'I have to do everything' and replacing it with the pursuit of 'the right thing, in the right way, at the right time'.

As much as 80% of the value of your tasks lies in just 20% of the tasks themselves. Getting good at identifying which things are in the 20% is the skill, as opposed to running around looking busy but going nowhere.

Under Commit and Over Achieve

'Under Commit and Over Achieve'. Yes under commit. If you've ever been involved in sales in anyway you may have heard the term, 'under commit and over deliver' specifically with a service-based business.

Well, when it comes to personal commitments and getting things done, I find it best not to overwhelm myself. You may have observed this of yourself too.

A Harvard study found that you become progressively less productive the more time you work past eight hours in a single day. And more than five day working at that pace in a row reduces productivity. Henry Ford noticed this during the early years on the production line in his factories. You could say this is the law of diminishing returns.

So how can you get more done, achieve your goals, remain in flow and get back to brilliant?

By being more productive with the fewer things that you do commit to wholeheartedly. By under committing you're left with spare capacity and therefore not becoming overwhelmed.

The amount of flapping that goes on when you get overwhelmed can be huge. That's like driving round with the handbrake on, no matter how hard you press the accelerator pedal it's still hard on the brakes and the engine.

Body Bank Modifications

You took the *Body Bank Calculator* test and you added up your score. If you were in the 16-35 or 36 and over category here are some suggestions to modify your work-outs.

Moderate (16-35 score) - with a score like this your body is showing signs of stress, a movement away from balance.

You need something that will help you top up the *Body Bank Balance*.

Here are some suggestions:

- Modify your workout by cutting it in half.
  Make a 40 minute session 20 minutes.
- Add more stretching into your programme.
  Stretch at the end as well if you are cutting back
  the total amount of time, as mentioned above.
- Do core exercises instead of resistance training.
- Double your usual rest periods between sets of
  exercise.
- Switch resistance training for a gentle swim or easy jog.

High (36-85 score) With a score like this your body is showing more significant signs of stress, a greater movement away from a balanced point. You need something even more restorative that will help you top up the Body Bank Balance to pay off some debt.

Here are some suggestions:

- Take the day off exercise and take a nap
- Have an Epsom salts bath instead
- Do some Qi Gong
- Complete your stretches only
- Have a massage
- Go for a walk in nature. If possible get your bare feet
  on the ground.
- Do all of your normal exercises but at breathing pace.
  (If its too hard to complete one repetition using just one
  breath, slow down. Make each repetition last at least as
  long as it needs to with each breath.)

Making at Commitment to Yourself

You now have a list of prioritised, actionable items written down from all the information that you have read in this book. As I stressed before and I'll stress again, information really is useless unless its put to work and it works for you.

So how can you make the list you made previously start to work for you? Daily practice and commitment to yourself! In the Chinese philosophy of Taoism they commit to doing a Gong when they want to master a new practice, move blocked energy and restore balance to the body, mind and spirit. A Gong is 100 days continuous practice of a specific task for small amounts of time.

By committing to a small task every day for 100 days and then ticking it off on a sheet, counting up to 100 ticks, you generate an abundance of the neurotransmitter Dopamine.

Dopamine is a key tool for you to use and understand when it comes to boosting your energy, improving your body shape and eliminating chronic aches and pains. Each time you achieve a small goal or tick an item off of your 'to do list' you get a hit of Dopamine.

When we eat we get a hit of dopamine. It also focuses us on our goals and is highly related to visual stimulus. That is why its very useful to use a tick sheet to record your progress of lifestyle change along the way to your 100 days. When you can actually see the accumulation of ticks building you get a shot of Dopamine. The more you do the more Dopamine is built and just like an addiction to something that detracts from you health and wellbeing you chemically get 'attached' to the new more beneficial habit that you have chosen.

This is the whole reason why I talked earlier about making small commitments and getting to the point where they are in maintenance mode.

If you are used to getting a hit of Dopamine and feeling great each day you do 10 minutes of stretching thats a fantastic lifestyle improvement.

It could be any of the tasks you have written down. Which ever one it is make a commitment and follow it through.

You might think 100 days sounds quite overwhelming, in which case I would recommend a 30 day commitment to begin with. The same physiological benefits take place in the short term, such as the small releases of dopamine, so you can build your new habits in 30-day chunks instead.

Client Case Study

Here's Tracey Burnette talking about the experience of being coached.

"I first met Adam in December 2010 when he approached me to operate his practice from Club Twenty-Two (the personal training gym I own). A number of extremely stressful incidences had occurred over the previous two years and my weight ballooned, I aged 20 years in 12 months and developed chronic nerve type pain in my left leg about 20 minutes after lying down, which created insufferable insomnia and subsequently a whole range of other health problems.

"I saw various specialists including strength and conditioning coaches, physiotherapists, acupuncturists, osteopaths, neuro-medical doctors and a whole range of other experts providing a wide range of advice and treatments - none of which worked for me.

"Having discussed my own personal health problems, one day Adam summarised the situation in one word 'fear'. Through Adam, I realised that all the treatments I had previously had were 'band aids' and nobody had got to the root cause of all my problems, consequently nothing changed for long. From my own observation, people can waste time and money and continue paying an 'expert' to fix them, without ever considering why the problem keeps returning.

"In my case, I decided to take a long hard look at myself and take more responsibility for my health.

"Adam's consultation forms seemed a little overwhelming at first, due to the time commitment to complete, so whilst travelling home from work each day, I broke it down into 20 minutes a day and finished them in two weeks. Adam said my forms were the best completed forms he had ever seen because I answered each section with total honesty.

"Adam impressed me from the first time I met him. Although unassuming, he is extremely knowledgeable, professional and believes in giving responsibility to his clients regarding their health and wellbeing rather than attempting to 'fix them'.

"Most importantly he carries out in depth assessments, leaving no stone unturned, listens to his clients concerns and creates a truly bespoke plan.

"Adam spoke a lot about the importance of having core values.

"The most difficult question for me to answer was, "If time or money were no object, how would you spend your days?" I suspect a lot of people would struggle to answer this question and like me, lost sight of their core values a long time ago, if they really had them in the first place. Most of us try to comfort ourselves with buying 'stuff' we don't need, abuse alcohol, drugs (recreational and prescriptive), over eat, don't exercise and constantly stress about all the above and more.

"I realised I could never be truly happy and fulfilled until I decided what would make me happy (core values) and had a maintenance plan to reach that. This became part of my daily life.

"Under Adam's guidance, I have dealt with and continue to deal with my own 'demons', (self-sabotage) and understand the importance that human beings are physical, emotional, intellectual and spiritual beings and to deny any aspect, rather limits our potential.

"My exercise routine fits around what I can consistently maintain (no more than 20 minutes in total) per day, with no hard core exercise routine. Because of my high levels of stress, the main priority was to bring the energy levels down to reduce the 'chaos' in my own body and head.

"Adam pointed out that exercise is actually a stressor, so if somebody's body is already under a lot of stress then hard exercise is the worst thing they can possibly do to lose weight.

"I do not profess to be an expert in many things but I believe my nursing qualifications, my knowledge, skills and experience in the health industry mean that I am proficient in assessing what makes a great personal trainer, exercise coach, corrective exercise specialist and health care practitioner.

"Adam helped me consistently gain better results than any other expert I have worked with in 25 years."

Results:

- I look better (younger) than I did 8 years ago, before I 'aged' 20 years.
- I feel more relaxed and a lot less stressed.
- I no longer have chronic pain, but if it does flare up, I know the reason why and deal with it.
- I am learning to play the piano and guitar, which I always dreamed of, but believed I was too old to commence.
- My personal life is much happier.
- My business is more successful.
- I lost 35lbs/16kg in weight over an 18 month period without this being my main objective.
- Dropped 2 dress sizes.
- Significant reduction in blood pressure.

Thank You

Thank you for taking the time to read this book.

Please remember this book is only as good as what you do with the ideas in it. Take some time to revisit chapters that you felt drawn to and take action.

Complete all the exercises and prioritise the actions that you are taking away from the book.

I sincerely hope *Back to Brilliant* helps you to make improvements in your health and wellbeing as these principles have for me.

One last thing

If you think Back to Brilliant
is about food and exercise,
you've missed the point.

What it's really about is uncovering
your most authentic self.

References

- Chek P, 1999. *Advanced programme design.* Correspondence course, Chek Institute, San Diego, CA
- Chek P, 2003. *How to eat, move and be healthy.* Chek Institute, San Diego, CA
- Chek P, *Holistic Lifestyle Coaching Level 2.* 5-day training course. Organised by www.chekeurope.com
- Chek P, Holistic *Lifestyle Coaching Level 3.* 6-day training course. Organised by www.chekeurope.com
- Cohen K, 1997. *Ken Cohen's guide to healthy breathing.* Audio book, Sounds True, Boulder
- Lane E, 2014. *Retune, rebalance, regenerate - The art of energy healing.* 2 day workshop, London
- Sears J.P, *The art of coaching.* Teleseminar series. www.innerawakeningsonline.com
- Sears J.P, 2014. *Living beyond self sabotage.* 2-day workshop, London
- Sears J.P, *Negative side of positive thinking* Online. www.AwakenWithJP.com/articles/negative-side-to-positive-thinking
- Sears J.P, *Piercing the seduction of your goals.* Online. www.AwakenWithJP.com/articles/piercing-seduction-of-your-goals/
- Sears J.P, *Reclaiming your power.* Online. www.AwakenWithJP.com/articles/reclaiming-your-power/
- Sears J.P, *Why is healing painful?* Online. www.AwakenWithJP.com/articles/why-healing-is-painful
- Wallden M, 2008. *Chapter 9.* Naturopathic Physical Medicine, Churchill Livingstone, Edinburgh
- Wolcott W Fahey T, 2000. *The metabolic typing diet.* Broadway Books, New York

About the Author

Adam Cox is the owner and head coach of *Movement Lifestyle. Movement Lifestyle* deliver 100 day mind and body transformational programmes for men and women 40 and over who want more energy, a better body and freedom from chronic aches and pain.

Having suffered with his own health challenges, resulting in an unnecessary operation, Adam wanted to find out more about what was going on, for himself. He began to study health and fitness with the *Chek Institute* who are world leaders in Corrective Exercise and Holistic Health.

Today Adam is a mentor for the Chek Academy students going through the training.

Adam believes that even the most complex of health challenges have their roots in simple lifestyle imbalances, compounded over time.

This is why he wrote his first book, *Back to Brilliant.*

What Next?

Are you ready to learn more about how these simple but incredibly powerful steps can help you:

- Move beyond sabotage
- Gain clarity with you diet
- Move with grace and ease
- Look fit and feel healthy again

The workshops

Adam runs a number of powerful workshops to bring these ideas to life, to test drive them so you can walk away with some new tools. Please register your interest at:

www.movementlifestyle.com/worskhop

Please stay in touch

Web   *www.movementlifestyle.com*
Facebook   *www.facebook.com/movementlifestyleuk/*
Instagram   *www.instagram.com/adampaulcox/*
Twitter   *www.twitter.com/MovementLife*

Lightning Source UK Ltd.
Milton Keynes UK
UKOW06f1330180816

280904UK00011B/200/P